American Cars in Europe,
1900-1940

ALSO BY BRYAN K. GOODMAN

*American Cars in Prewar England:
A Pictorial Survey*
(McFarland, 2004)

American Cars in Europe, 1900-1940
A Pictorial Survey

BRYAN GOODMAN

Foreword by KIT FOSTER

McFarland & Company, Inc., Publishers
Jefferson, North Carolina, and London

LIBRARY OF CONGRESS CATALOGUING-IN-PUBLICATION DATA

Goodman, Bryan, 1933–
American cars in Europe, 1900–1940 : a pictorial survey / Bryan
Goodman ; foreword by Kit Foster.
p.   cm.
Includes index.

ISBN 978-0-7864-2250-0
softcover : acid free paper ∞

1. Automobiles, Foreign—Europe—Pictorial works.
2. Automobiles, Foreign—Europe—History.
3. Automobiles—United States—History.
4. Automobile industry and trade—United States—History.
I. Title.
TL55.G65   2006   629.222094'022—dc22   2005032527

British Library cataloguing data are available

©2006 Bryan Goodman. All rights reserved

*No part of this book may be reproduced or transmitted in any form
or by any means, electronic or mechanical, including photocopying
or recording, or by any information storage and retrieval system,
without permission in writing from the publisher.*

Front cover: 1925 Packard Eight in the Alps near Garmisch on the
German-Austrian border. *Back cover:* The author with *(clockwise from
upper right)* his 1900 Benz, 1926 Amilcar and 1913 Sunbeam

Manufactured in the United States of America

*McFarland & Company, Inc., Publishers
Box 611, Jefferson, North Carolina 28640
www.mcfarlandpub.com*

ACKNOWLEDGMENTS

It is the quality and range of photographs that give this book its appeal. One cannot now thank the photographers of 100 years ago or congratulate them on their manipulation of heavy, glass-plate cameras, which so often gave a sharpness and quality that later cameras with small negative size do not match. Searching out these wonderful photographs has given me the pleasure of correspondence with new friends across Europe. Most of these new friends are members of the Society of Automotive Historians (based at 1102 Long Cove Road, Gales Ferry, CT 06335-1812 USA).

In the UK, Colin Rogers has been a valuably knowledgeable friend for the later American cars, as has Malcolm Jeal for the early ones. Help in the form of pictures has also come from Nick Baldwin, Alec Duncan, John Dyson, James Fack, Robert Grieves in Scotland, Tim Harding, Mark Morris and Stewart Skilbeck.

In France, my longtime friend Claude Rouxel is joined by Halwart Schrader and Antoine Vendiesse to be thanked, and the Collection Roger Viollet is to be acknowledged.

Thomas Ulrich in Germany, Petr Kosizek of the National Technical Museum, Prague, in the Czech Republic, and Trygve Krogsæter in Norway are all friends who have so kindly helped.

I went to Belgium, where Philippe Casse of the D'Ieteren Gallery of Brussels was kindness itself, as were Raoul Thybault and Monsieur and Madame Jacques Kupélian.

From Switzerland came photographs from Ferdinand Hediger and my longtime Amilcar friend Robert de Boer, plus one from the Swiss Car Register, Effretikon, Zurich.

I corresponded all over Europe with mixed results, but there can be no doubt that Sweden was trumps. Per-Börje Elg and Motorhistoriska Sällskapet in Sverige must be joined with Georg Magnusson, Stig Nyberg and Jan Ströman to receive my warmest thanks.

vi Acknowledgments

These friends and many others have been so encouraging and generous with their time and their pictures. Regrettably, the original photographers of so long ago must all now have gone; but they have left us these pictures to enjoy.

I hope that this pioneer motorist and photographer may be allowed to represent all those unknown photographers of long ago whose pictures have permitted us all to enjoy the photographs in this book. I only wish we could acknowledge them more personally.

TABLE OF CONTENTS

Acknowledgments v

Foreword by Kit Foster 1

Preface 1

Adams 7	Duesenberg 71
Anderson 8	Durant 75
Argo 8	Duryea 77
Auburn 9	Essex 78
Brough 12	Falcon-Knight 82
Buick 13	Ford 83
Burford 29	Franklin 101
Cadillac 30	Graham-Paige 104
Chalmers 42	Grant 106
Chandler 44	Harley-Davidson 107
Chevrolet 46	Hudson 108
Chrysler 53	Hupmobile 112
Cord 58	Imperial 120
Crowdus 63	Jensen 121
Daniels 64	Jewett 121
DeSoto 65	King 122
Detroiter 67	LaSalle 123
Diana 68	Lincoln 126
Dixie Flyer 68	Locomobile 130
Dodge 69	Marmon 132
Dort 70	Marquette 136

Table of Contents

Matford   137
Maxwell   138
Mercury   141
Moon   142
Nash   144
National   146
New Orleans   147
Oakland   147
Oldsmobile   151
Overland   153
Packard   157
Peerless   166
Pierce-Arrow   168
Plymouth   171
Pope-Toledo   173
Railton Terraplane   174

Red Bug   176
Regal   177
Reo   178
Scripps-Booth   180
Spacke   182
Star   182
Stewart   183
Studebaker   184
Stutz   191
Thomas   194
Westcott   196
Westinghouse   196
White   198
Wills Sainte Claire   200
Willys-Knight   202
Winton   204

Index   205

Foreword

Although Germany is usually recognized as the birthplace of the internal combustion automobile, it was France that first gave rise to a credible motor industry. The German, British and Italian industries grew more slowly, but until 1908 Europe was easily outproducing the nascent U.S. automobile business.

The United States overtook Europe in automobile production that year and has never looked back, but for some reason has never been recognized as an exporter of motor vehicles. American cars were regarded as crude in comparison to European machines, and France held the lead in vehicle exports right up until the first world war (although Britain was the leading buyer of imported automobiles).

The outbreak of war in Europe changed all that. European factories were diverted to munitions manufacture, in the words of the head of the German Daimler company, "the war was a huge glutton whose favorite dish was motor vehicles." The mechanized army was coming of age with trucks, tractors, tanks and buses.

But not with automobiles. The French taxis of the Marne notwithstanding, the passenger car was of limited value in combat, so European production ground to a halt. Not so in the United States, where war came late (April 1917), and hastily planned restrictions were never fully implemented. American automobiles, of necessity, then gained a toehold in Europe. They were found to be robust, reliable and cheap, so much so that tariff restrictions were enacted against them. In Britain, the so-called McKenna duties, named for the Treasury Secretary, placed a one-third penalty on all imported motorcars and parts, but this failed to cool the infatuation. No less a figure than Herbert Austin drove a Hudson Super Six, with which he was reportedly very pleased.

Thus began what might be called the golden age of the American car in Europe. This "world car" drew overseas assembly operations, and the local content helped to reduce the duties. While not exactly threatening the European auto industry, the American car became commonplace on the streets of the Continent, the British Isles and Scandinavia. This held true until war again consumed the world, this time affecting the American auto industry as much as the European one.

When peace returned, the goalposts had shifted. American cars had grown too big and hungry for austere postwar European pocketbooks, and there was too little hard currency to buy them. Europe, particularly Britain, had to export or lose its industry. Fortunately, small European cars became fashionable in parts of the United States, and the golden age somewhat reversed. The "world car" of postwar times has become a common shell or platform designed by the multinationals—General Motors, Ford and Chrysler—and tailored to local conditions in each country of sale.

Bryan Goodman's superb collection of period photographs, augmented by the archives of other collectors, demonstrates just how popular the American car was in Europe and shows how much their owners enjoyed them. It was an age of motoring that shan't come again.

Kit Foster

PREFACE

The story of the car divides neatly to the two sides of the Atlantic. It was Carl Benz (only in the last 50 years have the Germans changed him to Karl) who first made an internal combustion-engine car in 1885 in Mannheim, and he was closely followed by Gottlieb Daimler in Stuttgart. Daimler had already had a go at making a motorcycle, but his first car was a horse buggy to which he fitted steering and inserted an engine. However, Benz built his machine from scratch; it worked, and he and his wife made journeys in it. He soon fitted his production cars with four wheels rather than three and rotated the single-cylinder horizontal engine through 90 degrees so that the flywheel became vertical, putting an end to the sideways shaking of the vehicle at idle.

Daimler's 1885 machine was only experimental; he still had to create a whole vehicle and he then went on improving his product until in 1900 Europe saw the first Mercedes, a vehicle enormously ahead of the by then antiquated Benz.

I have sometimes thought that it was my bad luck, in 1956, to find a 1900 Benz rather than a 1900 Daimler, but it was actually good luck: At the age of 23, I could manage the little Benz but could not have tackled the Daimler/Mercedes.

In Britain the Government thought it knew best (as it still does today) and prevented any motorcar development. In 1865 an Act of Parliament that became known as the "Red Flag Act" decreed that any mechanically propelled vehicle had to have a minimum of three men in charge, one of whom had to walk in front carrying a red flag. If a vehicle journey was to be limited to the speed and range of a pedestrian there was no market for a car, should one go to the trouble of making one. The only vehicle likely to be encountered by the household's pony and trap was a traction engine towing perhaps a threshing machine, a living van and a water cart. Such a snorting road train would still frighten horses today. The Act was repealed in October 1896 and it is to celebrate the emancipation that British enthusiasts of motor history still celebrate the London-to-Brighton Run every November.

At the turn of the century, British roads were paved with stones. They became broken into sharp flints by iron-tired horse wagons and sprinkled with broken horseshoes and bent horseshoe nails, not a mixture to welcome the arrival of inflated tires. It was not just broken horseshoes and iron-shod wheels that caused a nuisance. Everyone on or near a highway was subject to the stuff that comes out of horses. In hot, dry weather the acrid ammonia-laden dust covered hedgerows and roadside gardens as well as cars. In wet weather it was a white slimy mud that stuck to anything and everything. But at least Britain's towns and villages were not far apart. American ones were much wider spread and there were no roads outside towns, which made travel in wet weather almost impossible and forced all vehicles to adopt the same wheel tracks as horse wagons.

During the century's first decade there was great change. The Americans got into their stride making big powerful cars and a few smaller ones. Britain made smaller cars and a few big ones.

Both world wars took a severe toll on the European industry, with steel and material shortages and bombed buildings. Peace brought newly released servicemen with their demobilization grants, often new driving permits and hopes for a new life. The shortages of cars meant that some dreadful motorcars (marketed by men equally optimistic for a new life) could easily find buyers, a state of affairs that did not last long. The twenties brought both sides of the Atlantic to crisis, though the changes were more sudden and much worse in the United States. Only some of the very strongest and best, and leanest, of the mass producers made it in Europe so the number of manufacturers was decimated. All this brings us to the date for the end of this book.

Like my previous book, *American Cars in Prewar England*, this one has given me great pleasure to prepare. My own collection of original photographs may be extensive, but I needed input from friends old and new across Europe to put this one together. Unfortunately, in some countries I had no luck at all in acquiring photographs. I am undecided whether this is because some countries did not import many American cars or because automobile history is just not of interest in those countries. The national representation is thus perforce haphazard, as is the depiction of the makes. How could one have expected to receive photographs of a 1901 Michigan and a 1904 Imperial, for instance, and to have a Marmon and yet omit some household names?

My thanks to many friends are listed on another page, but I must pay tribute to American friend Kit Foster, past president and one-time holder of most other offices in the Society of Automotive Historians. He has kindly written a foreword, vetted my photographs and text and generally tried to keep me on the right path. In England, Colin Rogers must be thanked for sharing his 1930s knowledge and Malcolm Jeal for his early car expertise. Contact with these and all those listed elsewhere has given me a most pleasurable time.

Now it is for the readers to enjoy these period photographs of cars, some common and some rare, before 1940.

Bryan Goodman
February 2006

ADAMS

Top and above: E. R. Hewitt of New York started business in 1906 making single-cylinder "Little Touring Cars" with the engines under the seat and false hoods. He supplied engines, transmissions and axles from elsewhere in New York to A. H. Adams at Bedford in England, who marketed the Adams car from 1905 through 1914. It was only the cars of the first couple of years that were based on the Hewitt, but the foot-operated epicyclic gearbox created the Adams slogan "Pedals to Push, that's all."

In the lower photograph, actress Louise Closser sits at the wheel of an Adams, but it is more than likely that she was posing for the photograph and was not able to drive at that time. The front view shows LN-883, a late 1906 London-registered car.

ANDERSON

Above: It is surprising that the Anderson Motor Car Company of Rock Hill, South Carolina, in business for only ten years from 1916, should have a satisfied customer in Denmark in 1919, as shown here. Anderson engines were from Continental and many other parts were by outside suppliers. Anderson's forté was its coachwork, including a convertible roadster, though this car is a two-seat roadster.

ARGO

Left: This car was built in 1914/15 by Benjamin Briscoe, but he made it in France as the Ajax with friction drive and in Jackson, Michigan, as the Argo with shaft drive. This one lived in Norway, but it was not powerful enough for Norwegian conditions. *(T. Krogsæter)*

AUBURN

Above: An Auburn Sedan 6-66 with London registration the only giveaway as to its location.

Above: This French-registered Auburn 115 convertible sedan of 1928 may be British owned to judge by the uniform of the chauffeur and the club badges, but the location is France.

Top and above: This cabriolet Auburn, again seen in France, must be the family's replacement for the 1928 sedan shown in the previous photograph as it has a similar badge-bar line-up. The cabriolet top did not fold away into the body but still allowed the rumble seat to be opened. Note the golf bag door behind the right-hand door.

Above: A French advertisement for the Auburn, 1930.

Above: The ultimate Auburn, the 852 supercharged Dual-Ratio Speedster was the last of the American boat-tail style. One is shown here competing at a concours d'élégance at Cannes on France's Mediterranean coast ahead of a Delage.

BROUGH

BUICK

Above: Only four years after the incorporation of the Buick Motor Company, this fascinating car arrived in Norway. The car is a Model F, current in 1906 and 1907, still with central chain drive but now with a full depth radiator allowing all the water circulating to be cooled and thus obviating the need for an additional water reservoir. The gas tank was now beneath the hood and the two-cylinder horizontally opposed engine was still beneath the front seats.

In 1909 Norwegian coachbuilder Carl Heffermehl made this body, and the car was sold to be used in Lillehammer, the winter Olympic town, as public transport. *(T. Krogsæter)*

Opposite, bottom: George Brough had been a maker of top quality motorcycles in Nottingham, England, when in 1935 he introduced the Brough Superior car, which was based (like the Railton) on a Hudson chassis. The more usual body was a drop-head coupé by W. C. Atcherley of Birmingham. It had automatic chassis lubrication and a hydraulic four-point jacking system. Using the Hudson six-cylinder engine, it did not have the performance of the Railton which mostly used eight-cylinder units.

14 *Buick*

Above and left: Buick cars sold before 1914 in Britain and bodied there were sold as Bedfords and then as Bedford-Buicks. These two are both badged as Bedfords; the Lincolnshire registered (DO) Model 35 two-seater, above, is what one would expect in England, but the other car has wire wheels and is a French picture of a Model 29.

Buick 15

Above: The heavy horizontally topped hood of this just postwar Buick E-44 allied to the low placing of the headlights overpowers the British drop-head body. The car was registered in Oxford.

Above: A British-built two-seater. The chassis is the lightest Model H-44. The photograph was taken in front of Fort Augustus Abbey, Inverness-shire, Scotland, in 1921 or 1922.

Top and above: Two brand new Buick five-passenger cars with right-hand drive. They are both photographed in London with obviously British coachwork. To the author's English eyes both cars are improvements on the square sedans of the Flint product, despite the "graceful rounded lines" promoted by the company for 1921. The wire wheels give both cars a lighter feel, as does the rear fender sweep of the all-weather with vee-windshield. The limousine (top), which is on a longer chassis and has a three-faceted windshield, is displaying a Surrey dealer's trade license plate and was destined to be sold via the Oatlands Park Motor Co. Ltd. garage at Weybridge in Surrey.

Above: This Norwegian taxi driver is visibly proud of his 1923 Buick with pelmets decorating every window. The car may be of local manufacture, but the "California top" used to provide winter warmth in an open car may dispute this. *(T. Krogsæter)*

Right: The English gent with pipe and spats should be proud of his car as it is apparently one of only four to be exported. It is a Buick Master Six four-passenger Coupé Model 25-48. Oval quarter windows are fitted below false landau irons, which have to assume an uneasy shape to clear them. The sun visor appears to be covered in the same rubberized fabric as the top, with the opera lights giving a final smartness.

Above: The five-passenger Buick Master Six Sport Touring collects its lady passengers from La Grande Cascade Restaurant in the Bois de Boulogne outside Paris circa 1926.

Top and above; A 1926 Buick Standard Six Sport Roadster is seen in the south of France. Below, a Standard Six Sport Touring sets out from Rylstone, near Skipton in Yorkshire, with a load of fare-paying passengers who were photographed before they set out and would be offered postcards on their return—hence the number on the photographer's negative.

Opposite, bottom: A little dog waits in a 1926 Buick Standard Six with English-built two-seater plus rumble seats body. On the running board is a battery box, and ventilators resembling those on board ships have been rotated to be extractors. Sidelights and English headlights are fitted, probably now of twelve volts. The bustle-like boot is reminiscent of the 1920 Cadillac on page 35.

Top and above: A family picnic in rural France with a 1928 Buick Standard Six Coach in the background. The lower photograph shows the ladies in what the British call a doctor's coupe. It may be British, but France is the location of the photograph.

Above: From the Berne area of Switzerland hails this 1928 Buick Standard Six Coach with 23.4 SAE h.p. engine. It was the base model sedan.

Above: Fit for King Haakon VII of Norway is this fine Buick "Master Six" Touring of 1929, probably pictured in Stavanger. The semaphore direction indicators on the sidelight brackets are European, and surely the car looks so much more elegant on wire rather than wooden wheels.

Buick remained a most popular car until World War II, after which few American cars were sold and small European cars were again on the roads. For a time only East European cars could be bought without a permit, so many Skoda, Moskvitch and Wartburg cars were seen in Norway. *(T. Krogsæter)*

Les marques de voitures particulières circulant sur nos routes

1912	Nombre	1929	
Martini (CH)	539	Fiat (I)	8866
Pic Pic (CH)	332	Citroën (F)	5101
Renault (F)	217	Buick (USA)	2841
Peugeot (F)	148	Ford (USA)	2445
Turicum (CH)	140	Chrysler (USA)	2267
Fiat (I)	139	Peugeot (F)	1916
Clément-Bayard (F)	130	Chevrolet (USA)	1843
Rochet-Schneider (F)	126	Renault (F)	1724
Tribelhorn (CH)	121	Essex (USA)	1342
De Dion Bouton (F)	117	Ansaldo (I)	1043
Zedel (F)	109	Nash (USA)	1038
Brasier (F)	107	Whippet (USA)	834
Fischer (CH)	105	Amilcar (F)	832
Stella (CH)	101	Mathis (F)	777
Sigma (CH)	84	Martini (CH)	747
Opel (D)	83	Hupmobile (USA)	741
Darracq (F)	79	Packard (USA)	710
Bianchi (I)	76	Delage (F)	706
La Buire (F)	75	Dodge (USA)	684
Mercédès (D)	69	Studebaker (USA)	656

Above: This little cutting from Switzerland records that in 1912 there were no American cars in that country. By 1929, however, over half the makes were American, with only Martini still a Swiss maker.

Opposite, bottom: A modernist Buick advertisement (a credit line at lower left reads "Ettler") that followed a very successful exhibition in Sweden in the summer of 1930. The top line translates "See it—and you will drive it. Drive it—and you will want to own it." *(P-B. Elg)*

Above: Posing at the time of the 1929 Paris Motor Show, which was then in the Grand Palais on the Champs Elysées, is this Buick Series 40 four-door sedan. The disc wheels, sidemount and bumper were accessories, but the radiator shutters were a 1930 introduction.

Above: A French advertisement of 1930.

Above: A series 50 Buick Eight of 1933. New fenders, the abandonment of wooden wheels and a 2¼ inch overall lowering gave the 1933 models a new look behind the new V-grille. The cabriolet body by Carrosserie Langenthal AG of Berne in Switzerland, under license from Alexis Kellner of Berlin, is the same as that on a 1933 Hupmobile in this book on page 118. *(F. Hediger)*

Above: Hans Osterman was a Swedish representative for General Motors supplying Cadillac, LaSalle and Buick. Osterman established a partnership with Nordberg coachbuilders of Stockholm, who bodied a number of these cars. This is a 1933 Series 50 Cabriolet.

In the early thirties, separate rear trunks were gradually incorporated into bodies, and here is one whose integration is retarded by its color treatment. *(P-B. Elg)*

Above: King Edward VIII reigned only in 1936, abdicating to marry American divorcée Mrs. Wallis Simpson. The king purchased "his and hers" Buicks in 1936. This is her Model 80 at a seaside town in France where the couple lived from the date of the Abdication as the Duke and Duchess of Windsor.

Opposite, bottom: A 1934 Buick now converted into a van stands between a Wolseley (left) and a Morris Series II Sixteen-Six or Eighteen-Six saloon all equipped with white painted bumpers and blacked out headlights which were a wartime requirement when car lighting was very restricted. They appear to be the fleet of the Watford, Hertfordshire, "Area O" ARP (Air Raid Precautions) during World War II.

Above: Photographed in Portugal is a 1938 Buick Special four-door Touring Sedan with its trunk back. It was the company's most popular car in 1938, and the accessory dual sidemounts gave the car class but were not cheap.

Above: After abdicating the throne in 1936, King Edward VIII, now Duke of Windsor, went to live in France. The duke had a Buick Model 90 limousine in 1936, and here is his 1938 Buick in France. Note that free-standing French Marchal headlights have been fitted.

BURFORD

Top and above: Mr. H. G. Burford had founded Milnes-Daimler at the beginning of the century and in 1914 became agent for Fremont-Mais lorries of Fremont, Ohio. Burford trucks had four-cylinder 29 h.p. Buda engines with central-change gearboxes, shaft drive and a capacity of two tons. These vehicles were sold in England and the United States as Burfords until 1917 when the American company was sold.

Both these trucks must have had first world war military careers. The canvas-roofed truck is seen at West Norwood, South London. The other has become a test rig for the Smith-King paraffin (kerosene) carburetor, an example of which is shown on the knee of one of the group.

CADILLAC

Above: The date is 1904 and these are the first three taxicabs in Stockholm, Sweden. On the left is a 1903/4 Cadillac, and on the right a 1904 Model B Cadillac. Between them is a Michigan, a real rarity. There were several makes of car called Michigan. The car shown here is made by one of two companies that were based in Kalamazoo. *(P-B. Elg)*

Left: Mr. Axel Nilsson owned this Cadillac as a taxi in Stockholm, Sweden, and the car is photographed in the Haga Park outside Stockholm in May 1907. Single-cylinder Cadillacs were used in many Swedish cities; some had locally built closed bodies.

A LADY'S TOUR.

THE 9 h.p. single-cylinder Cadillac driven by the lady at the wheel (Miss W. F. M. Ousby-Trew) has recently travelled over 2,000 miles through Wales. The load was as shown, with luggage at the back, and no *chauffeur* was taken. The route was Upchurch, Guildford, Salisbury, Wantage, Banbury, Stow-in-the-Wold, Gloucester, Whitchurch Hill (much surprise was shown at the car successfully negotiating this gradient), Abergavenny, to Crickhowell. From this centre runs were made in all directions, including Hay, the Golden Valley, Hereford, the Wye Valley with the Forest of Dean (stiff gradients); over the Brynmawr Hills to Swansea Eistedfodd, and through the whole of the Gower Peninsula including Kettle Hill; the Birmingham Waterworks at Rhyader (a magnificent trip); the Brecon Beacons, Sishowy, and Caerphilly; the triangle of castles, viz., Grosmond, *via* the Hand Hill, Skenfirth, White Castle; the direct road from Brecon to Builth, by the Chapels and "Tumble-down-Dick" Hill, perhaps the finest road (1,200 ft.) for panoramic scenery. Thence the course lay *via* the Abergwesyn Valley (splendid scenery all the way, but three fords, one of 60 yds.) to Llanwyotdd, and through the Sugar Loaf Pass to Llandovery for the sheep-dog trials. This road (1,000 ft.) most nearly resembles an Alpine pass of all those traversed on the tour.

Leaving Crickhowell the adventurous driver proceeded through Carmarthen to Tenby, and on to St. David's for the cathedral, *via* Newgate and Clova—quaint villages. The grand coast scenery through Fishguard, Carnarvon, and Aberystwyth was next visited. A *détour* was made from the coast road south of Newquay to visit the rocky shore at Llangranog resembling Clovelly. Then the itinerary was Trawscoed, Devil's Bridge, Machynlleth, Coris, the Pass of Tal-y-llyn, Dolgelly, Trawsfynydd (very bleak), down the worst hill in Wales, viz., Maentwrog public road to Portmadoc, Beddgelert, Bettws-y-Coed, Llangollen, and thus to Shrewsbury, whence the tour was concluded *via* London.

Only on one occasion did the car turn back, viz., when attempting to get from Hay to Michaelchurch by St. Paul's pilgrim road over Cusop Hill (1,400 ft.), as the road was too loose and rough. The worst road traversed was in the Gwaen Valley between Fishguard and Newport. Miss Ousby-Trew left the main road and came direct from Morvil to Ponfaen, through a swollen ford and up a shingle hill. The hotel accommodation, she writes, was, throughout the tour, as a rule good, sometimes excellent, and not expensive as compared with the cheaper. Petrol was obtainable at all sorts of queer places, including a jeweller's. The average pace worked out at fourteen miles an hour. The little Cadillac car appears to have behaved in an excellent manner right through this long and arduous test.

Above: This article reports a trip from Guildford (southwest of London) to Wales in a 9 h.p. Cadillac in February 1908 and the fact that it was driven by a lady. The car is surely a 1905 Model F.

Above: The registration archives of Inverness County Council in Scotland still have many of their records, so we know that ST-393 was a 20/30 gray-colored torpedo Cadillac bought by Captain Douglas of Cameron Barracks, Inverness, on May 15, 1912. He kept it less than a year and is not the man in the photograph. The car has a tax disc on the windshield frame, so this photograph dates from 1921 at the earliest. It was possible to buy steel disc wheels before World War I, but they were more often seen in the twenties.

L'arrivée du Président Wilson.

Above: After the first world war, the Norwegians found that large American cars were the most suited to hilly Norwegian roads, and from then on American cars dominated the market. Here, a 1918 Cadillac is brought out to work as a snow plow. *(T. Krogsæter)*

Opposite, bottom: The armistice ending the first world war was signed on November 11, 1918. In January 1919 the U.S. president, Woodrow Wilson, attended at the Palais de Luxemburg in Paris. Thirty-one countries were represented, but only the four major ones, France (G. Clemenceau), England (Lloyd George), Italy (King Victor-Emanuel II) and the United States (T. W. Wilson) finalized the treaties, the most important of which, the Treaty of Versailles, would be signed with Germany in June 1919.

Here, President Wilson arrives at the Palais de Luxemburg for a banquet in his honor on January 20, 1919, in a Cadillac—though his own car was a Pierce-Arrow.

Above: A Cadillac in Norway sports a local hood ornament: the trophy antlers of a caribou. *(T. Krogsæter)*

Above: A 1918 Cadillac Type 57 with the ninety degree V8 engine. The location of this touring is surely the south of France.

Above: From another picture of this car when less travel stained, we know that it had 1920 London registration. The Cadillac roadster has room for three in the front for this tour of Switzerland, so the rumble seats can be reserved for luggage while two more suitcases are strapped to the running board.

Above: The Sucreries and Raffineries of Romania ordered three Cadillac Torpedos for delivery in 1920 bodied by D'Ieteren Frères of Brussels and photographed in the Avenue Jupiter in Brussels, Belgium. This is the first of them, delivered on May 25, 1920. *(D'Ieteren Gallery, Brussels)*

Above: At the side of an English road is a London-registered 1925 Cadillac. This is the two-door, five passenger coach body, new to the Standard line in 1925 and the car is the V-63 Eight. Duco paint finishes were new to Cadillac in 1925 and allowed an eruption into no fewer than twenty-four color combinations that year.

Above: The King of Spain, Alfonso XIII, is carried in a 1927 Cadillac Series 314 dual-cowl phaeton. Only in 1927 did the radiator carry the little widow's peak in the radiator surround.

Above: One of the Cadillac agencies in Brussels, Belgium, in late 1927. In front of the showroom with the roof box is a Cadillac V8 sedan and behind it two LaSalles, new cars for 1928. *(Y. and J. Kupélian)*

Above, left and right: A Cadillac V8 of 1928 in the Bois de Boulogne, Paris. The occasion is a concours d'élégance on June 8, 1928, and this car is bodied by Parisian coachbuilder Saoutchik over the original Cadillac fenders and valance. Bumpers were standard from this year. The car won first prize for cabriolets at the concours.

Above: A Cadillac V8 sedan of 1928 is parked outside the garage of Guttman & Gacon at La Chaux de Fonds in the Jura mountains north of Neuchatel in Switzerland.

Above: This Cadillac 341-B of 1929 is bodied as a Coupé de Ville by G. Gangloff SA of Geneva. The engine was a V8 of 341 cubic inches (5,572 cc), and this is the first year the sidelights became fender mounted. This longer 152 inch wheelbase (the standard was 140 inches) was normally reserved for limousines or ambulances. The falseness of the landau irons is obvious as they would be unworkable, but they do allow for a good rear window length. *(F. Hediger)*

Above: Gustaf Nordbergs Vagnfabriks AB was Sweden's most famous coachbuilder. In 1930 Nordbergs built this elegant body on a Cadillac V16 chassis. During the early days of the 1930s there was little demand for expensive luxury cars in the Depression. With this picture arrived the following story:

"This Cadillac was unsold until 1934, when a wealthy publisher bought it. When he came to the Marble Halls (Marmorhallarna), the elegant showrooms of AB Hans Osterman, the GM dealer in Stockholm, he wore a simple and rather worn suit. When he stopped in front of the huge Cadillac asking for the price, the salesman told him that it was very expensive and suggested a Chevrolet instead. The publisher demanded to see the manager and bought the Cadillac for a reasonable price. He did not use it very much. Many years ago this one-off Cadillac V16 passed to a Swedish collector and is still a low mileage car." *(J. Ströman)*

Top and above: Alexis Kellner of Berlin were coachbuilders from 1910 until taken over in the thirties. There was no connection with Kellner Frères of Paris. This is the king of Sweden's 1931 Cadillac with crowned radiator cap and headlights. A crown is also fitted here in place of the license plate, though the car also had registration A22.

Below is a picture of an Alexis Kellner 1931 Cadillac on pre-delivery plate. It could even be the royal car if the wheels were to be altered. *(Both P-B. Elg)*

Above: For 1932 Cadillac continued with three engines of V8, V12 and V16 layout. This is the V16 with wheelbase of 143 inches and carrying convertible coupé body by Lancefield Coachwork of west London. This car does not have the golf bag compartment or the rear-hinged doors of its factory-made equivalent.

Above: A V8 Cadillac of 1934 with four-door convertible body by Gebrüder Tüscher & Co of Zurich, Switzerland. In this book there are also photographs of a Buick, a Hupmobile and a Packard of similar date and with tops springing from very low at the back. To cope with cold winters these tops were horsehair interlined, and wind- and watertightness were most important. The tops on Swiss and German coachbuilt cars usually folded poorly and remained higher than windscreen level when so folded. *(F. Hediger)*

Above: By 1939 it was already becoming difficult for a coachbuilder to be effective on an American car. The radiator design of this Cadillac carries into the fenders so that the front half of the car has to remain unaltered. French coachbuilder Franay bodied this 1939 Cadillac coupé shown here at a concours d'élégance in Paris. Despite the month being June, the model appears to be holding a fur coat. *(H. Roger Viollet, Paris)*

CHALMERS

Above: A British advertisement for Chalmers in 1914.

Opposite, bottom: Chalmers-Detroit became Chalmers in 1910 and from 1914 included a Six, which quickly became the only model until the 1922 takeover by Maxwell, which was itself already a Chrysler subsidiary. This tourer is in Norway. *(T. Krogsæter)*

CHANDLER

Above: This Chandler Big Six of 1927 bears a German (Hanover) license plate. Built in Cleveland, Ohio, 1921–1929, this make was well thought of. Chandler made their own six-cylinder engines, adding eights in 1928. *(H. Schrader)*

Opposite: This Chandler advertisement appeared in the *Swiss Touring Club Revue* special edition for the 1927 Geneva Salon. *(F. Hediger)*

CHEVROLET

Above: Chevrolet called this the Superior Sedan in 1923. Front and rear bumpers were available as extras. This one on the wrong end of a towing "ambulance" is no longer superior, and the damage is perhaps more than bumpers could have protected. Three of its wheels are off the ground, so why a "driver" was necessary is beyond comprehension. Vigo Motors were London agents for the make.

Chevrolet 47

Above: On show at the Amsterdam salon in Holland in early 1928 are the new Chevrolet National Fours, larger cars with full crown fenders. The bullet-shaped headlights, now normal on Chevrolets, were much more familiar in Europe, where drum-shaped lights were never used. In the center of the stand is a two-door coach and on the right a four-door sedan. Belgian Englebert tires are fitted. *(Y. and J. Kupélian)*

Opposite, bottom: At General Motors' first premises in Belgium at Fortuinstraat, Antwerp, in 1925, sedans and tourings await buyers. During 1925 a bar was fitted between the headlights which reduced vibration of both the lights and the fenders. *(Y. and J. Kupélian)*

48 *Chevrolet*

Top and above: A London furniture removals company chose to use a 1½ ton lorry with trailer in 1929. It is a Chevrolet Six Series LQ now fitted with disc wheels. The giant General Motors had been wanting to expand into Europe and in 1925 took over Vauxhall at Luton. Chevrolet commercials were good sellers in Britain through the twenties but this is its "Six for the price of a Four" which quickly became Luton's best seller and led to the new British commercial, the Bedford. Below is the same model Chevrolet but this time timber hauling in Vörmland, Sweden. *(S. Nyberg)*

Above: Swedish taxicab regulations specified eight seats, necessitating a long wheelbase, as shown in this 1931 Chevrolet. *(P-B. Elg)*

Above: The M Series 1½ ton Chevrolet truck of 1931 used a new 157 inch wheelbase and twin rear wheels. This one was based in the south of France, and it is believed to be a wine tanker with pump as its load.

Above: A French advertisement for the 1932 Chevrolet Six Series BA convertible cabriolet with rumble seat. This very attractive car outsold Ford by over 70,000 cars in 1932.

Above: The Geneva Salon in Switzerland in 1933 showing that year's Chevrolet range. Center foreground is the two-door sports roadster and behind it a Master Eagle sedan. On the right are a two-door coupé and a four-door town sedan. *(Y. and J. Kupélian)*

Opposite, bottom: What a smart turnout on a Swedish lake in 1932. The ladies are warmly clad in their Chevrolet DeLuxe Sports Roadster. Two rumble seats and the deluxe features were the chromed hood ports and trumpet horn. The six-cylinder engine had 194 cubic inches. By 1932 almost all Chevrolets were closed cars. These ladies are probably only posing for the General Motors Nordiska advertising department. *(J. Ströman)*

Above: Radiator covers were normal in Sweden in winter. This local grocery store in Tärnsjö, a small village in Västmansland Iän county, uses a 1935 Chevrolet ½ ton panel delivery. New for 1935 was Chevrolet's eight-passenger wagon using the same basic body shell. *(P-B. Elg)*

CHRYSLER

Above: The Chrysler Series 75 chassis is the base for this convertible by Uhlik of Prague, Czechoslovakia. Chrysler ran two cars in the French 24-hour Le Mans Race in 1928 and they came in third and fourth; in 1929 they were seventh and eighth. *(National Technical Museum, Prague)*

Opposite, bottom: Parading in England, but obviously on their way to France in 1941, are these two Chevrolet one ton BN catering vans. The sign reads "Church Army," "Mobile Canteen for HM and Allied Forces."

Un croisement anonyme!

CE N'EST PLUS LE MOMENT D'ACHETER UNE CARTE ROUTIÈRE

Vous poussez votre moteur: ce n'est plus le moment de penser à l'huile. Vous êtes à 50 kilomètres de votre dîner et il est 9 heures du soir. Votre appétit demande à votre moteur un effort soutenu et des reprises nerveuses. Si celui-ci s'en montre incapable, ce n'est plus le moment de penser au graissage.
C'était avant qu'il fallait régler cette question une fois pour toutes en adoptant le type de Mobiloil indiqué par le Tableau de Graissage affiché chez votre garagiste. Mobiloil possède exactement le corps qui convient pour protéger les surfaces frottantes contre l'usure et résister aux hautes températures et aux pressions élévées.
Le type de Mobiloil exactement approprié à votre système de graissage sera distribué d'une manière uniforme dans tous les organes à graisser. Votre moteur demeurera jeune, il fournira l'effort que vous lui demanderez.
Adoptez le type qui convient à votre moteur puis... oubliez votre graissage, nous nous en sommes occupés pour vous.

Pensez dès maintenant à **Mobiloil** en bidons de 2 litres repris vides Frs. 2,50

Opposite, top: The world's first Winter Grand Prix for cars was arranged in 1931 by the Royal Automobile Club of Sweden. The number of racing cars was small. Most of the competitors drove American cars, more or less modified. Here is a 1930 Chrysler Series 70 roadster at a tricky part of the 30-mile-long circuit. The driver is Clemens Bergström, who finished in third place behind an Auburn and a Chrysler Imperial. Four such winter events were held. In 1932 a Ford Model A, equipped with a Record cylinder head, won a sensational victory, and in 1936 a supercharged Graham was winner of the class for standard cars. *(J. Ströman)*

Above: A Belgian chauffeur and his 1931 Chrysler Model CM Six sedan. Wire wheels were standard, but dual sidemounts were extra.

Opposite, bottom: This French advertisement for Mobiloil dates from 1932, but the pair without a map have a Chrysler 66 Roadster from 1930.

Above: A Chrysler Imperial of 1932 convertible by Graber of Wichtrach, Bern, Switzerland. *(Swiss Car Register, Effretikon, Zurich)*

Above: Uhlik of Prague built the convertible body for this 1932 Chrysler. While the fender line gives the car cohesion, the low V-screen, landau irons, angular trunk and poor looking bumpers make for a slab-sided car that one could hope was a one-off. Scuttle-mounted sidelights were also outdated by 1932 and these have another peculiarity: they lift with the full length hood! *(National Technical Museum, Prague)*

Chrysler 57

Above: A Chrysler four-door sedan in Spain. The bumpers and headlights at least are not standard.

Above: This 1934 Chrysler Model CB sedan was the longer of the two conventional Chryslers still being sold, the rest of the range having the new Airflow styling. Over 17,500 of this most popular model were sold. Sidemounts and rear luggage rack were extras. This one is seen at Dover in April 1939 being loaded aboard the SS *Prince Charles* at the start of a continental holiday.

CORD

Top and above: E. L. Cord made the Auburn and the Duesenberg at Auburn, Indiana, and in mid–1929 he introduced this car, the Cord L-29. This was the first front-wheel drive passenger car to be volume produced. The Lycoming straight eight engine was used, but turned to have the fly wheel at the front. It was such an immediate success that the makers could not cope with the orders received, but problems with the car, followed by the stock market crash, cooled demand very quickly.

In October 1929 the Cord was launched at the London and Paris shows. The car at top here is the standard cabriolet at the latter event. Below is another cabriolet competing at a concours at Cannes in the south of France. The Cord was of such low-slung and exciting appearance that with stock coachwork it won many concours d'élégance, beating cars with coachbuilt bodies. The car behind is a French Delage.

Above: French advertisement for Cord, 1930.

Above: Standing next to his 1930 Cord is Isaac Grünewald, one of Sweden's best known artists, particularly recognized for stage décor. He called his car "Fågel Blå" (Blue Bird). Although the new L-29 Cord was expensive, had front-wheel drive, and was unknown, the Swedish agent Philipsons sold more than fifty before the economic depression.

The double-breasted suit, spats and hat at a jaunty angle are eclipsed by a Cord L-29 cabriolet front-wheel drive. American cars were not beautiful to European eyes but the long, low Cord L-29 was a very different proposition and won many concours d'élégance in its first year of 1930. *(J. Ströman)*

Opposite, top and bottom: Two fancifully lengthened European design studies, the first from Castagna of Milan, Italy, for a dual-cowl phaeton and the second from Saoutchik of Paris, intended to be a longer chassis for a "city cabriolet." Note that the striking waist moulding is repeated on the separate trunk.

Above: What a surprise to the author to receive in the mail a photograph of the 1931 Cord L-29 LaGrande. The photograph came from Sweden! The LaGrande name was used by Cord's experimental coachwork department, and this one-off car in maroon and cream is believed to have been bought by Paul Berns, husband of screen actress Jean Harlow. The car had drink holders inside the doors. The skirted fenders were inspired by aeroplane aerodynamics, and the hood louvers were curved in the style of Duesenberg, a company in the same stable. Having been displayed at the New York Motor Show in 1931, the car came to France and won first prize at a concours d'élégance in the Bois de Boulogne that summer. Here it is in later life in front of a Hispano-Suiza with the white-wall tires no longer white. *(J. Strömän)*

Opposite: American actress Winifred Vernon was playing in London in 1902 when she bought this little Crowdus electric car. Late in 1902 when this article was produced the Crowdus company had already given up. On this car the steering tiller also controlled speed and braking.

CROWDUS

[No. 21, October 15, 1902.] THE CAR. 249

A NEW ELECTRIC CAR:
MISS WINIFRED VERNON AND HER RUNABOUT.

MISS WINIFRED VERNON, a charming American actress who made her name in the best of the Frohman productions on "the other side," is visiting England, and opened at the Surrey Theatre last Monday with a play entitled "The London Fireman." In one of the scenes a victoria was to have been drawn on to the stage by a pair of horses, but Miss Vernon is a progressivist and will have nothing less modern than an electric automobile.

The car used is her own, and the first of its kind to be imported into England. It is a Crowdus, a dainty runabout invented by a Chicago engineer of that name. She came by her possession in rather a curious way. Walking in Charing Cross Road with her manager, she noticed a smart little car standing not far distant from Wyndham's Theatre. She spoke to the driver, who turned out to be Mr. W. A. Crowdus himself, and he directed her to the Fischer Motor Vehicle Company, the owners of the patents. Within half-an-hour she had signed a cheque and the carriage was hers.

We dropped into the offices of the Fischer Omnibus

handle, and may be operated with one hand. A child of ten could drive it with perfect safety.

The Crowdus has the flexible running gear, silent transmission, a piano box body, automatic electric and double acting mechanical brakes, and can be run at any speed from three to twenty miles an hour. It will cover fifty miles without being recharged. The weight is only 1,000 lbs.; and, of course, being an electric car, is practically vibrationless. Mr. W. A. Crowdus is a "bright man," as the Americans would say, and Mr. Simms holds a high opinion of his abilities. The Fischer Company have purchased the Crowdus patents for the world, believing that in two or three years' time there will be no more widely used car. Mr. Simms does not fear the muchly-boomed Edison storage battery, and says that it will have to go through longer and more serious tests before its vaunted qualities are proved. As for Signor Marconi's invention, if as good as reported, it is the very battery the Fischer Company are wanting; but Mr. Simms lays a delicate stress upon the "if."

Photo, by] MISS WINIFRED VERNON AND HER NEW CROWDUS CAR *[Lafayette*

DANIELS

Above: The expensive V8 Daniels was only made from 1915 to 1924 at Reading, Pennsylvania, by the man who had previously been president of Oakland Motor Car Company. A big and expensive car it was made in small numbers mostly to special order. Of the few remaining today, this one is still in Norway. *(T. Krogsæter)*

Opposite, bottom: A 1929 DeSoto Six, Series K, sedan acts as backdrop, and perhaps wind break, to three English ladies having a picnic tea. In the thirties DeSotos were badged in Britain under the Chrysler name.

DeSoto

Above: The DeSoto stand at the Portuguese Motor Show at Oporto in 1929. The previous year, Walter Chrysler had bought Dodge and created two new makes of car, Plymouth and DeSoto. The DeSoto had a six-cylinder engine of 2,866 cc and went well. In its first year of production (1928/29), it had great success at over 80,000 cars with sales the best for any new U.S. maker up to that time. *(Y. and J. Kupélian)*

Above: Here is a Belgian registered DeSoto Series K of 1930. The sidelights have been brought forward to the fenders and the wheel nuts hidden behind the chrome hubcaps. A golf bag door on the other side gives access to the rumble seats. *(Y. and J. Kupélian)*

DETROITER

Above: The Detroiter was an assembled car from Detroit. It was marketed in England as the Royal Detroiter, and in 1914 the engine was a 2,811 cc four-cylinder Continental. Much of the production may have been sold in England, but the make only lasted until 1917.

Opposite, bottom: The occasion is the Brussels Motor Show in December 1934, but the historian's interest in the picture will not be the three very new DeSoto Airflows but the occupiers "D.S." of the other half of the stand. The German Stoewer was made at Stettin in northeast Germany. The company was declining in 1934 and did not survive the war (nor did Stettin, being renamed Szczecin in Poland). "D.S." was the name chosen by Monsieur Dewaet hoping to sell Stoewers in Belgium, but the 1934 show was its only appearance.

Today we appreciate that all seats should be within the wheelbase of a car and that the engine is well placed between the front wheels. In 1934 a long hood and shorter body were necessary for an elegant appearance. Here the grille and hood length of the Airflow are sacrificed to passenger space, and these are the short 9 ft 7½ in. wheelbase cars, whereas the Chrysler Airflow Custom Imperials used 12 ft 2 in. The Airflow was DeSoto's only offering for 1934. Built-in headlights, wider front seats (allowed by the narrower running boards) and the V-windscreen were also all new—too new for the public, and both DeSoto and Chrysler had to offer more traditional models beside the Airflows in 1935. *(Y. and J. Kupélian)*

Diana

Above: The Diana was a subsidiary of the Moon Car Company introduced in 1925. The prestigious radiator was copied from that of the Belgian Minerva car. The cars were named for Minerva, goddess of wisdom, and Diana, goddess of the moon and hunting. This photograph comes from Switzerland.

Dixie Flyer

DODGE

Above: Dodge was a well-respected make in Sweden throughout the twenties, but by 1932 when this eight-cylinder car was made, less than one percent of production was of convertibles. Here, outside the studios of Svensk Filmindustri, Sweden's greatest prewar film company, is Isa Quensel, one of their popular actresses. *(J. Ströman)*

Above: The Swedish company Philipsons was for many years the largest importer and distributor for makes including Cord, Graham, Dodge, DKW and Mercedes-Benz. This line-up in the spring of 1938 is to celebrate the new Dodge assembly plant at Augustendal, just outside Stockholm. The sign on the first car reads, "I am Number One from the car factory in Augustendal." *(P-B. Elg)*

Opposite, bottom: Louisville, Kentucky, may not be where one would expect motor cars to be made, and most were sold in the southern states. However, here is a 1920 Dixie Flyer that has found its way to Switzerland, and some also came to Britain.

DORT

Above: A 1923 Dort. The Dort was made in Flint, Michigan, and in only ten years (1915–1924) over 100,000 cars were sold; this one reached Jönköping in Sweden in 1924. J. D. Dort was friend, one-time partner and protégé of William Crapo Durant, who joined Buick in 1904 and then founded General Motors in 1908. *(S. Nyberg)*

Opposite, top: The Duesenberg was introduced for 1921. This Model A roadster with cutaway doors carries Berlin, Germany, registration. Fred Roe's book *Duesenberg—The Pursuit of Perfection* tells us that an agency in Berlin sold several Model As. *(T. Ulrich)*

Opposite, bottom: When the Duesenberg "J" was launched into Europe at the London Motor Show at Olympia in October 1929, it was this Murphy bodied right-hand drive chassis that was exhibited and described as having a "black and silver all weather body."

Duesenberg

Above: In 1931 this Duesenberg Model J was owned by a garage in Berlin Halensee, an area at the end of the Kurfürstendamm where the most expensive car retailers were to be found. It is a dual-cowl phaeton by LeBaron, then of Detroit, which was the most often seen open Duesenberg body style. *(T. Ulrich)*

Above: This Duesenberg is thought to be the Model J shown at the Paris Salon in October 1930 where it was sold to Prince Nicholas of Romania. The car is a convertible victoria by Parisian coachbuilder Letourneur and Marchand, with Grebel headlights and door handle placed centrally. The picture shows a Letourneur and Marchand car on the harbor front at Cannes with a concours trophy on the running board. The car beyond is a French Voisin.

Above: Obviously this is a Model T Duesenberg, but that central door handle was the early thirties signature of Parisian coach builder Letourneur and Marchand. This two-door "faux-coupé" was commissioned by Spanish nobleman the Marquis de Portago, father of Alfonso de Portago a grand Prix driver in the middle fifties. The interior upholstery was in beige calfskin, and inside the doors there were handles at both ends to provide access to passengers in both the front and backseats. The body style was built on more than one hundred Delage chassis but also on Buick, Bugatti, Delahaye, Renault and others. Another Duesenberg J was built for Prince Nicholas of Romania and is shown on the previous page.

Above: A short wheelbase Duesenberg with body credited to Van Den Plas of Brussels seen here at the Salon of Brussels in December 1934. It seems that there are questions still unanswered concerning this most singular car, both as to how complete the Van Den Plas contribution was and that the car has not been heard of since. *(Y. and J. Kupélian)*

Above: This may be the only Duesenberg bodied by d'Ieteren Frères of Brussels, Belgium. It was delivered to Mr. Ades on October 1, 1935. It is car 2548, J519, and has a smooth, attractive and balanced line for such an enormous car. The size and weight of the door must have been considerable as four hinges are used. *(© D'Ieteren Gallery, Brussels)*

Opposite, top: In 1920 the Royal Dutch Shell Group sold gasoline in the Netherlands under the trademark "Autoline." Here at the Garage Alberts in Hilversum, a 1919 Durant receives some of this spirit. *(T. van Wijk)*

Opposite, bottom: A 1922 Durant in the British countryside. It must be brand new as it is being used on "trade" license plates.

DURANT

76 Durant

Above: A Durant of about 1923 outside a British army barracks. W. C. Durant created General Motors in 1908 but was forced to resign in 1910. He was back in charge in 1915 but was out again in 1920. Undaunted, he created Durant Motors Inc. in 1921.

Above: The Norwegian flag is in the background behind this 1924 Durant four-cylinder model A-22. The model would shortly be fitted with four-wheel brakes and have disc wheels and balloon tires as standard. *(T. Krogsæter)*

Opposite, bottom: The Duryea was the first "manufactured" U.S. internal combustion engined car, and thirteen were built in 1896. Two Duryeas were entered in the original London to Brighton Run in November 1896. From 1902 until 1906 Duryeas were also made in Coventry, England. This is a 1902 advertisement from *Car Illustrated Magazine*.

Above: A Dutch family is on holiday in Portugal in 1929. The figure with the hat and proprietorial pose in the center of the group is the chauffeur, and on the left is Mr. José Machade, the first owner of the car. The location is the south of Portugal on a small ferry over the River Gudiana. The 1929 Durant 60 has a six-cylinder side valve Continental engine, and its third and current owner is the lender of the photograph. *(T. van Wijk)*

DURYEA

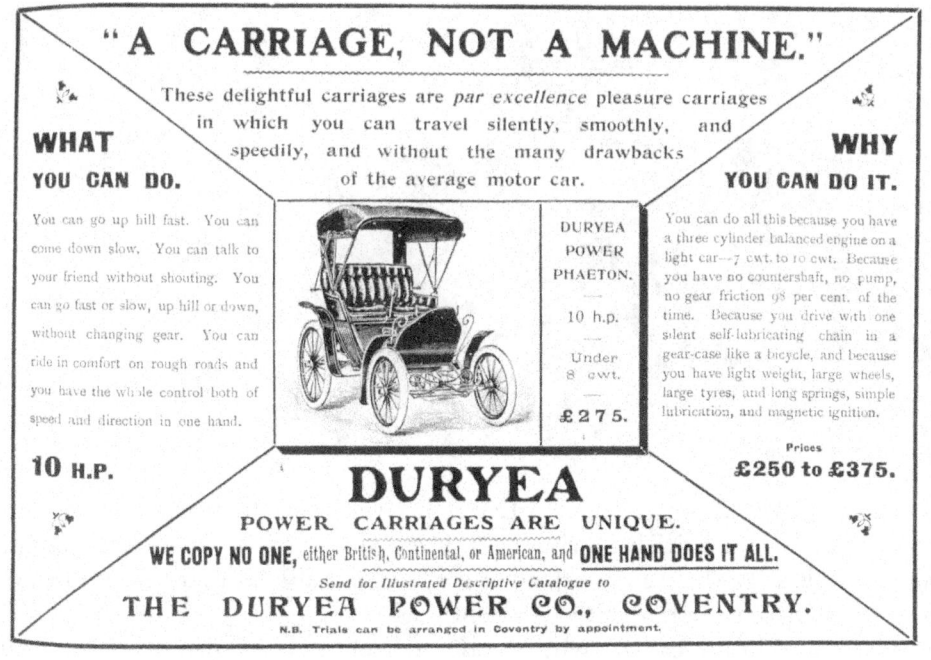

Essex

Top and above: What fun to have an Essex that was registered SX! The car dates from 1920 and has a British touring body fitted. SX was issued by the County Council of West Lothian in Scotland, but it was possible at that time to register a new car anywhere so perhaps it was intentional.

Below is a similar car but with wooden wheels and in Norway. *(T. Krogsæter)*

Above: This 1925 Essex two-door coach has German registration with the letter I indicating the Bautzen area of Saxony. A little girl is proud to pose on the fender. The direction arrow, worked by a Bowden-style cable to rotate the arrow from within the car, was a novelty fitting that had a short popularity in the twenties.

Above: The driver is famous Swedish actor Gösta Ekman, photographed in his Essex tourer in Stockholm in 1927/28. *(S. Nyberg)*

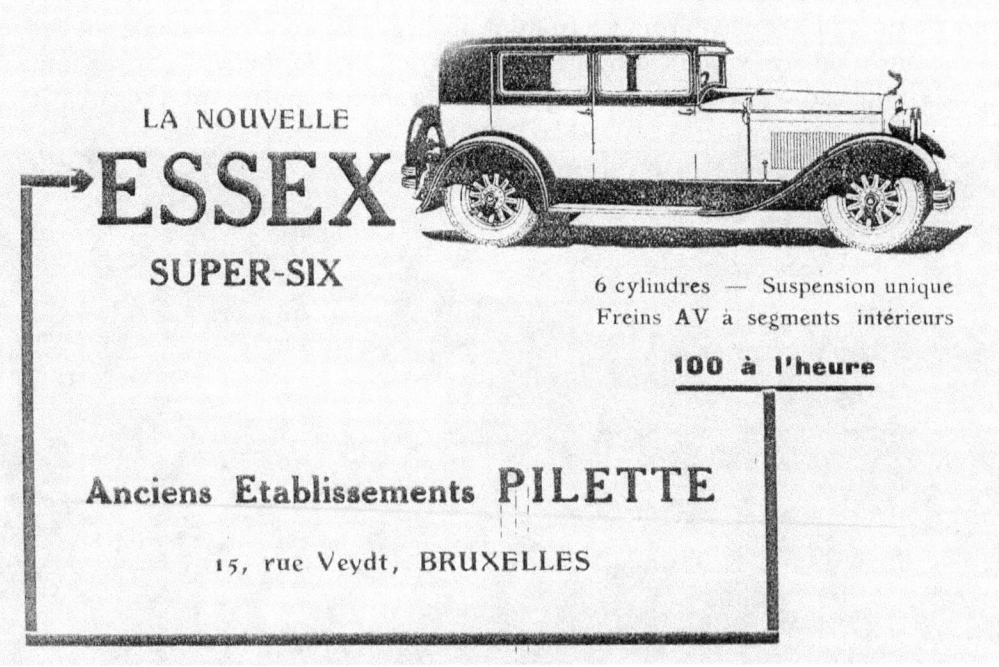

Top and above: The 1928 Essex sedan had an inline six engine with cast iron block. The front and rear bumpers were extras. This one was photographed at Bridgwater in Somerset in 1929, and in 1930 the Belgian advertisement (below) appeared in the *Englebert Tyres* magazine. *(A. Vendiesse)*

Top and above: The Essex Challenger Town Sedan of 1929 was imported to England for local assembly for sale at a price thought "astonishingly low" of £295. Its engine was a six cylinder of just over 2½ liters. The radiator shutters could be opened from the driver's seat. The location of this photograph is behind the London offices of Temple Press, publishers of *The Motor* weekly magazine.

The lower picture shows the sea front at Penarth on the south coast of Wales, near Cardiff. It is out of season to judge by the warm clothing, and only a 1929 Essex is parked.

FALCON-KNIGHT

LA DERNIÈRE CRÉATION
DE
Willys-Knight :
La 12 HP
FALCON-KNIGHT S/S
SLEEVE VALVE SIX

Freins intérieurs aux quatre roues.

La FALCON-KNIGHT possède toutes les qualités de la merveilleuse WILLYS-KNIGHT. Son moteur (6 cylindres sans soupapes KNIGHT à 7 paliers), bien que n'ayant qu'une cylindrée de 2 litres 450, donne à la voiture une vitesse de plus de 100 kilomètres à l'heure et lui permet d'ignorer les côtes qu'elle gravit sans effort.

Par l'élégance et le confort de ses carrosseries, la FALCON-KNIGHT ne le cède en rien aux voitures plus coûteuses.

La Willys-Knight à la portée de tous

FALCON-KNIGHT Six, modèle Sedan.

12 litres 1/2 aux 100 kilomètres.   FC 120

REPRÉSENTANT GÉNÉRAL POUR LA BELGIQUE ET LE GRAND-DUCHÉ :
PALAIS DE L'AUTOMOBILE
88, boulevard Adolphe Max, et 54, rue du Pont-Neuf

Téléphone : 146.48   BRUXELLES   Télégrammes : Wilauto

AGENCES ENCORE DISPONIBLES.

FORD

Above: Little could these Norwegian men have imagined that they were sitting in a make of car that, within ten years, would become the most popular in the world. This is a Model R Ford of 1908, at the end of which year the Model T would be introduced. *(T. Krogsæter)*

Opposite: The Falcon-Knight was meant to be an independent make but was actually marketed by John North Willys alongside the Whippet Six. The make, with its factory at Elyria, Ohio, lasted only through 1927/28. Surprisingly this advertisement appeared in 1930 in the *Englebert Tyres* magazine. It is amusing now to note that the top line advertising "the latest model" could also be translated as announcing "the final model" from Willys-Knight! *(A. Vendiesse)*

Above: The first motor races in Sweden were held on frozen lakes. This one is just outside Stockholm. Even the brass monkey adorning the radiator has turned to question the sanity of this Model T driver without windshield or snow chains. The body and rear mudguards indicate that the car may be of English manufacture. *(J. Ströman)*

Above: A lineup of Model Ts requisitioned for ambulance duty in the first world war. The soldier here appears to have been in sole charge. His name is Lyddiatt and before the war he had been the chauffeur of a big Daimler chain-driven landaulette for Lord Elton of Headington in Oxfordshire. The cars appear to date from 1916, the year before the United States joined the war and very many Fords would be sent to Europe.

Right: British advertisement for Ford, from *The Autocar*, 3 April 1915.

Opposite, bottom: Even before the first world war, the Ford T was a common sight on British roads, including as a commercial vehicle this one of a toy maker in the city of London. From 1911, Fords were built near Manchester, England.

This page, top and bottom and opposite, top: Two Ford T's by coachbuilder Privat of Dijon, France. The timber-bodied pick-up has a carrying capacity of 500 kilos, but it also has removable rear seats and an overall folding top. The French call this style "Normande." Then there is a tourer "torpedo commerciale" which could be used as a tourer for going to church on Sunday, but by removing the rear seat it could become a general carrier for vegetables or livestock during the week.

Above: The date is May 1, 1918, a little over five months before the end of the first world war. The location is a factory at Batignolles in Paris, where a young French soldier sits at the wheel of one of three Ford Model T's prepared for military service.

Above: The location is northern France, near Arras, but the car was registered in London in 1919. The back of the picture has the comment, "One of many such incidents. On road between Doullens and Albert, France."

Top and above: Two coachbuilt "Ts" from France in the early twenties. Above is a brake with side curtains made by A. Rousset of Lyons on the larger TT one ton chassis, and the lower car a sedan by Lion de Belfort in Paris with opera lamps set forward of the windshield and inverted "V" fenders. The styling is very rectangular, but the date is too early for it to be on the Weymann principle.

Opposite, bottom: The body of this Ford circa 1920 was made in Manchester, but for what? The left-hand front door does not have a handle, the running board is of wood, rather than the original pressed steel, and the rear doors seem a bit small for a hearse. It must still have made quite an impression to see such a rounded rear in the early twenties.

Above: A stripped T-Ford with locally made or proprietory speedster body in a competition in Gothenburg, Sweden, in 1927. In the background is an Italian Fiat tourer. *(S. Nyberg)*

Opposite, top and bottom: This car is surely based on a Model T, though the front axle is dipped and the radiator is labelled "Auto Cab." The occasion must be a trial or demonstration of taxis in Paris. Note also that the gas tank is now filled from the top of the bulkhead, a feature that would be standard on the Model A from 1928. The lost movement in the various controls, not least the steering, must have made for a very unpleasant drive.

    The idea of a cab that placed the driver on top was not new. As the sketch demonstrates, a common Hansom cab design in nineteenth-century London placed the cabby in the same location. This was not as impractical as it looks. When harnessing up, the cab was heavy on the horse, but when the cabby was seated the vehicle was balanced. The passengers had easier access and their weight was not important as it was over the axle. A hatch in the roof allowed the fare to instruct the driver and presumably also to pay him at the end of the journey.

Above: Surely built in Europe is this Ford T tonner with heavy duty rear wheels and tires. It seems to be built as a bus but in use as a works hack at DKW, the German motorcycle maker of the twenties who became the largest motorcycle maker in the world. Cars were introduced for 1929, and DKW joined Audi, Horch and Wanderer in 1932 in the formation of Auto Union.

Visible inside this Ford are a bicycle and a motorcycle. The translation of the sign is "Sooner or later everybody drives a DKW."

Above: January 1925 in Stockholm and the 30,000th Ford imported starts its journey around Sweden in one week (Ystad to Haparanda). *(P-B. Elg)*

Right: Prince Sigvard Bernadotte of Sweden in his Ford circa 1926. Registration 'A' is for Stockholm, and low numbers were reserved for the royal family and other officials. *(P-B. Elg)*

Opposite, bottom: A Model T Ford landaulette operating as a Paris taxi. It is fitted with disc wheels. The location is Paris circa 1925 and the photograph is captioned "l'auto-écraseur," which means something between roadhog and a mechanical fly swatter. From the earliest days there had been inventions for cow catchers on cars to pick up pedestrians. This photograph reassures us that the man hit by the car falls into a sitting position in front of the hood.

Above: The Motor Show at Dusseldorf in Germany in 1926, the last full year for the Model T Ford. The car was updated and restyled with new fenders, running boards, some bodies and hoods. The whole car was lowered about one inch, which may not be obvious, but the result is to show a much better balanced vehicle helped by the polished radiator. The Fordson tractor, visible beyond the truck on the left, had been introduced in 1919 in America. *(Y. and J. Kupélian)*

Above: An AA one ton Ford truck is posed in France with what must be its new family of owners.

Above: The 1931 Ford 'A' DeLuxe Roadster is shown by three Belgian models. The roadster could have either a rear trunk or a rumble seat as here, and the cowl lamps and sidemount were standard on the DeLuxe model. *(Y. and J. Kupélian)*

Opposite, bottom: Outside the "Grands Garages de Bretagne" (Brittany) of Monsieur H. Matile. On the posts behind the cars are logos for (from the left) Chenard et Walcker, Delahaye, Delaunay-Belleville, Rochet Schneider, Delage, Ford and Rosengart. The cars in the line (again from the left) are two Rosengarts, two Chenard et Walcker, Delahaye, Delage, Ford Model A, two Delaunay-Bellevilles and a second Delahaye. The date must be 1928 or 1929.

Above: This Ford AA of 1931 is attached to a semi-trailer, an unusual arrangement for the time. Coder of Marseille made trailer units and containers for the transport of wine.

Above: A new Ford V8 Fordor enters service as a taxi in Budapest, Hungary. The tires are labeled as Englebert from Belgium, and the car has a limousine division behind the driver and a full length fold-back roof. The windshield is also less high. The body could well be by Gläser of Dresden, Germany.

The V8 was introduced in April 1932, and nearly 300,000 were sold in the year at a home price for the Fordor of $590, the same price as the previous year's four-cylinder Fordor. *(Y. and J. Kupélian)*

Opposite, bottom: Here on a German film set or advertising set is a 1931 Model A Ford with a German-made body and an A.D.A.C. (roadside recovery service) badge covering the Ford one. *(T. Ulrich)*

Left: "Hearty congratulations" is the message on this card, printed in Paris but posted and received in 1936 in Holland. The lady is in the advanced new V8 Ford announced in April 1932 at only $10 more than the four-cylinder Model A. This is the convertible cabriolet that could be had with either a trunk or a rumble seat. On some models the chromed spare wheel cover was an extra, and on this car the headlamps have been replaced by a pair of French Marchals. *(C. Rogers)*

Above: Miss Finland 1934 poses with a new Ford Model 40. The Ford V8 was introduced in 1932 as "the greatest thrill in motoring." It was in a 1934 Ford V8 (but a sedan) that bank robbers Bonnie and Clyde were killed in a sheriff's ambush. Clyde Barrow had even written a letter to Henry Ford in 1934 praising the Ford V8.

Opposite, bottom: Shown here is Prince Eugen, the youngest brother of the Swedish King Gustav V (1858–1950) and a very talented artist. He bought his first car, an Oldsmobile Curved Dash, in 1905 and soon became an early owner of a Ford Model T. During his life he used several open Ford cars as mobile studios for his outdoor work. The chauffeur had to see to it that curious people did not come too close to the prince and disturb him when he was painting.

This is the 1932 Model 18 V8 convertible sedan which sold at home for $650. Though it might have looked unusual in America, such retention of the door frames was common in Europe and was even seen after the war on the Citroen 2CV. *(J. Ströman)*

Above: Bodied by Uhlik of Prague is this Ford V8 of 1934, the year the one millionth Ford V8 was made. These mid–European convertible bodies were fully lined to cope with cold winters, and one can imagine how poorly this top would fold. *(National Technical Museum, Prague).*

Above: July 22, 1939, in Stockholm when Ford delivered its 100,000th car in Sweden. This car and other Fords visited Ford dealers around the country, where a 1939 Standard was called V8 Special and this one, a Royal de Luxe. *(P-B. Elg)*

FRANKLIN

Above: A 1920 Franklin in Norway. Perhaps an air-cooled car would have been sensible in a country with very cold winters that froze water in radiators. Four years later the American Franklin dealers pushed for a more conventional look which would involve a false "radiator," and this came for 1925. Franklin lasted until 1934. *(T. Krogsæter)*

Above: At Cannes on the Cote d'Azur, a Buick and a Franklin, both circa 1926, await their owners outside the Palm Beach Casino. *(C. Rouxel)*

L'AVION DE LA ROUTE

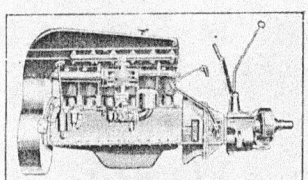

Vue extérieure du moteur de la Franklin.

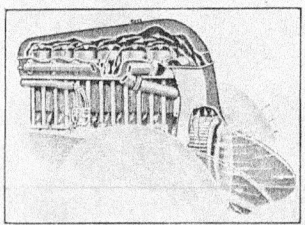

Coupe du système de refroidissement par air. Forcé par l'action d'une puissante turbine, l'air est envoyé sous un énorme volume à la tête des cylindres autour desquels il s'écoule entre les ailettes en cuivre qui les entourent. La quantité d'air est plus grande aux points où règne la plus haute température.

C'est ainsi que l'on peut caractériser la Franklin dont l'allure puissante et souple, la force de traction, l'ardeur à fendre l'air, éveillent l'idée de vol tant l'impression qu'on y éprouve diffère de l'ordinaire sensation de l'automobile.

Cette allure si spéciale de la Franklin, qui ne s'oublie plus une fois qu'on l'a connue, a été recherchée et obtenue par le constructeur grâce à un certain nombre de perfectionnements exclusifs tels que : suspension scientifique par 4 ressorts pleins elliptiques, freinés par amortisseurs hydrauliques à double effet d'une douceur idéale, faible poids non suspendu qui libère presque totalement la carrosserie des cahots de la route. Enfin, légèreté exceptionnelle due en partie au système de refroidissement par air extrêmement efficace qui, par la suppression des radiateur, pompe, canalisation, ventilateur, confère au châssis une légèreté considérable et diminue le poids mort.

Esssayez une Franklin, vous verrez que son surnom d'Avion de la Route n'est pas usurpé.

CONCESSIONNAIRE POUR LA FRANCE :
CHICAGO GARAGE, 24, RUE DES BELLES-FEUILLES, PARIS

FRANKLIN

Above and opposite: Two French advertisements for Franklins.

Graham-Paige

Le verdict de la clientèle

Série complète de six et huit cylindres. Quatre vitesses. Deux prises : une de ville, une de route.

GRAHAM-PAIGE INTERNATIONAL CORPORATION
DETROIT, MICHIGAN, U. S. A.

L'accueil enthousiaste que les usagers de l'automobile ont bien voulu accorder à la nouvelle série complète de voitures Graham-Paige démontre clairement la qualité exceptionnelle de cette production: Le chiffre des ventes pour l'exercice 1928, au moment de la clôture des formes de cette édition, accuse une augmentation de plus de 300% sur la même période de l'année dernière

Joseph B. Graham
Robert C. Graham
Ray A. Graham

Directeur Général pour l'Europe
SIDNEY H. DIMAN
18, Avenue Matignon
Paris

GRAHAM-PAIGE

DIVERS MODÈLES SERONT EXPOSÉS AU SALON DE L'AUTOMOBILE. STAND N° 76

De front avec le Progrès.

Modèle 615 ROADSTER

En 1929, Graham-Paige améliorant encore ses modèles, vous offre une voiture parfaite ayant toujours la supériorité de ses 4 vitesses (2 prises silencieuses.)
Venez l'essayer et vous apprécierez toutes ses qualités.

Joseph B. Graham
Robert C. Graham
Ray A. Graham

GRAHAM-PAIGE présente une gamme complète de carrosseries sur cinq châssis 6 et 8 cylindres (boîte spéciale 4 vitesses).

SALON DE L'AUTOMOBILE
Stand 22 (Grande nef)
Concessionnaires pour la France :
Établissements A. d'ANDIRAN, 44, Avenue des Champs-Élysées, PARIS
Téléphone : Élysées 08-96, 08-97, 08-98.

GRAHAM-PAIGE

Opposite and above: Two French advertisements for the Graham-Paige.

GRANT

Above: Photographed in Denmark in 1914 or 1915 was this smart new Grant. The company was started in Detroit in 1913 and eventually moved to Cleveland, Ohio. The startup team all had considerable motor manufacturing experience. The Grant was a tiny two-seat roadster on a 90 inch wheelbase, but it had a 12 h.p. water-cooled four-cylinder engine and should have stood out from the many cyclecars then being produced—but it didn't. The cyclecar bubble burst in 1915, but the Grant grew up to be a real car and survived until 1922. *(S. Nyberg)*

Opposite, top and bottom: For many years Harley-Davidson was one of the most popular motorcycles in Sweden. Most Harleys were in private hands, but many of these powerful machines were used as commercial vehicles like these, a 1930 and a 1934, equipped with spacious platform sidecar bodies. All were seen in the traffic of Gothenburg in the 1930s. *(J. Ströman)*

HARLEY-DAVIDSON

HUDSON

Above: If this is a 1922 Hudson Super Six with bell-shaped headlights and beaded edge tires, it predates by three years the company's introduction of the nickel-plated radiator shell. It is Bournemouth registered, and the landaulette body is by Bournemouth coachbuilder Martin. The body has much softer lines than the Detroit product.

Above: Hudsons of the early twenties with one right-hand and one left-hand drive. The registration plates are Belgian. The individual letters are attached to a frame, which is just as well as solid plates would have restricted air flow to the radiators. The scene appears to be a party readying for a day's motor outing.

Above: A British-bodied Hudson saloon of 1926. There is a bouquet of fresh flowers in the dashboard vase, but no tread on the tires!

Above: A 1927 Hudson Standard Coach two-door makes its way through flooding in England's Somerset Levels in the winter of 1932.

110 *Hudson*

Above: Santander is a seaport on the northern coast of Spain. All but one of the eight cars in this street scene near the Hotel Paris are American. From the left, they are a 1929 Hudson Super Six, a French Renault, a 1928 Essex Super Six, a 1929 Graham-Paige and 1927 Buick. In the distance is a 1927 Chrysler 70 and on the right a 1928 Chrysler Imperial and a 1929 Auburn.

Opposite: Swedish advertisement for the 1937 Hudson.

STILRENHET, PARAD MED KRAFT, GER SEGER ...

Hudsons sobra stil har slagit igenom — den är en vagn, som är modern år efter år.

Har Ni kört den nya graciösa och smidiga Terraplane — den körsäkra vagnen, byggd i Hudsons anda. Se den i dag!

1937 års Hudson är starkare ... lägre ... bekvämare ... rymligare ... den har plats för tre i framsätet. Allt är konstruerat med tanke på största möjliga säkerhet. Viktiga konstruktionsdetaljer är den styrda framaxeln, de hydrauliska bromsarna och Duplex förgasare, som betyder så mycket för bensin-ekonomien. Lägg också märke till "anti-imbildaren", den sätter Ni värde på i vårt klimat. Vi tillåta oss föreslå Er en provtur och demonstration. Vi stå beredvilligt till tjänst. Ring nu!

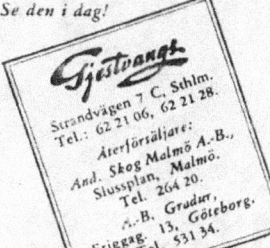

HUDSON 1937

— vagnen alla beundra

HUPMOBILE

Above: Registered with Bedfordshire County Council, England, in 1912 was this Hupmobile tourer.

Above: The "Tour de France Automobile" of 1912 included this four-cylinder 12 h.p. Hupmobile.

Top and above: Two 1913 Hupmobiles in France. The high headlamps were a Hupp hallmark.

A German Hupmobile advertisement from just before the Great War. *(T. Ulrich)*

Above: Fuel problems were felt across Europe in the Great War. This 1915 Hupmobile is fitted with a town-gas balloon in Norway. Wood fuel producer gas systems were much used in France, but elsewhere in Europe (including Britain) these town-gas bags were seen. *(T. Krogsæter)*

Above: Registered in Cornwall, England, is this 1923 Hupmobile tourer wearing a Royal Automobile Club badge.

Above: Actress Dolly Davies enjoys her 1929 Hupmobile Century Six Roadster registered in the Le Mans area of France. There are enough spectators to imagine a concours d'élégance, but there is no plaque on the car. The previous year, 1928, Hupp adopted styling as a feature using Murray bodies designed by Amos Northup, causing sales to soar, but in 1929 sales dropped again. *(C. Rogers)*

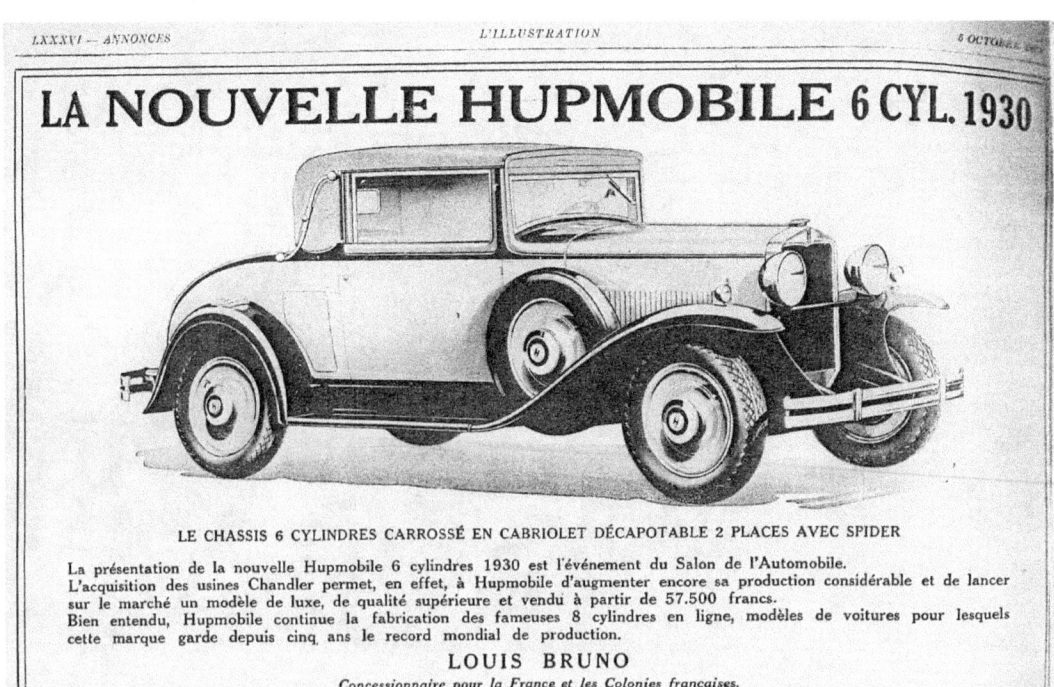

Opposite, bottom and above: Two 1930 French Hupmobile advertisements.

118 *Hupmobile*

Above: A proud lady glamorizes her Hupmobile Century Six of 1931 in Paris.

Above: Hupmobile Aerodynamics on a Norwegian sales forecourt. They are model 518-D six-cylinder sedans. *(T. Krogsæter)*

Opposite, bottom: A Hupmobile Six in Switzerland, a type K-321 six-cylinder of 1933 with cabriolet body by Carrosserie Langenthal AG of Berne, who built bodies on many American chassis. (See this body on a Buick on page 25.) Langenthals were licensed by Alexis Kellner of Berlin (not connected with Kellner Frères of Paris) to build drop-head coupes to Kellner design. *(F. Hediger)*

IMPERIAL

Above: From Columbus, Ohio, to Norway in 1904 seems a big step, but here it is, a 1904 Imperial 8 h.p. air-cooled twin. F. Hiorth was the Imperial sales agent in Christiana (now Oslo). Note the very long handles above the dashboard and the complete elliptic springs all around. The hood has been replaced with a poor imitation of a Franklin.

In 1904 this car was driven from Oslo to Sandefjord, the 100 mile journey taking four days. On the way, the F. Hiorth salesman visited Count Wedel Jarlsberg to try to sell him a car. He was apparently affronted by the din of the air-cooled engine and sent him away. *(T. Krogsæter)*

Opposite, bottom: The Jewett was named after H. M. Jewett, the president of the Paige-Detroit Motor Car Company, as a small six-cylinder companion to the Paige. Some 40,000 were made in the years 1922–1927, and this Touring with right-hand drive must be 1924 and in England.

Jensen

Above: Alan and Richard Jensen had produced some modified Ford V8s for the 1934 Tourist Trophy Race in Ireland and then made some specials over the next three years. Their Anglo-American venture took off in 1937 with Ford V8 or Nash straight eight engines. Columbia two-speed rear ends gave six forward speeds.

This 1938 saloon Jensen is from Jensen's own coachworks and is Nash powered with modified Ford chassis.

Jewett

Above: Winter's damage to the roads of Sweden begins to show with the melting snow, but the excitement was too much for the driver of this 1926 Jewett two-door sedan. *(P-B. Elg)*

KING

LaSalle

Above: The LaSalle was introduced in 1927. Here a 1927 phaeton of seven-manpower is maneuvered outside the Cadillac depot in Paris. The famous stylist Harley Earl was hired by Lawrence Fisher, president of Cadillac in 1927, to be stylist for LaSalle, General Motors' new make. The car Harley Earl most admired at the time was the Hispano-Suiza, and one can see this influence here, although the result is still totally American.

Opposite, bottom: A Swedish advertisement from *Motor* in 1920. *(P-B. Elg)*

Above: When students graduated from college in Norway it was the tradition to paint old cars with slogans, of which this 1929 LaSalle sedan would have been typical. Some of these cars then went to the scrapyard, but some were saved for eventual restoration. *(T. Krogsæter)*

Above: Seen in Belgium is this 1934 LaSalle four-door sedan. Parent company Cadillac's idea was to create the LaSalle as a model in between the Cadillac luxury make and the cheaper Buick. The LaSalle was introduced in 1927 only three years before the stock market crash, and by 1934, when this car was made, it had become neither a small Cadillac nor an adolescent Buick, but an up-market Oldsmobile. LaSalle finished in 1940.

Opposite, bottom: What a pleasure it is to see a European body really complementing an American chassis. AB Hans Osterman, the General Motors dealer in Stockholm, had a partnership agreement with coachbuilder Gustav Nordbergs, who made this attractive cabriolet on a 1930 LaSalle—to this author's eyes a better balanced effort than the factory managed, which is not always the case. *(J. Ströman)*

LINCOLN

SCHWEIZER TOURING-CLUB 33

LINCOLN

RAFFINEMENT

La Lincoln a été conçue pour ceux qui peuvent choisir dans la multiplicité des offres ce qu'il y a de mieux, l'objet qui représente l'ultime expression de l'ingéniosité humaine.

Elle vous donne le meilleur en qualité à un prix modéré. Ce résultat est rendu possible par la précision de la fabrication telle qu'elle est pratiquée par les maîtres reconnus dans l'art de réunir hommes, matériaux et ressources mécaniques sans rivaux dans le monde entier.

Élégance de ligne, douceur d'action, vitesse dans l'accélération, facilité de conduite, telle est la Lincoln, avec laquelle aucune autre voiture ne peut se comparer.

La Lincoln est la perfection de ce monde; demandez-nous un essai, il sera plus éloquent que toute littérature. Où que vous soyez, le nécessaire sera fait.

Honorez notre Stand No. 75 de votre visite au Salon de l'Automobile à Genève

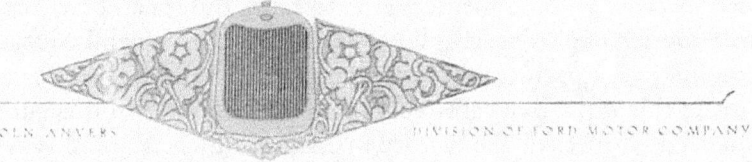

AUTOMOBILES LINCOLN ANVERS — DIVISION OF FORD MOTOR COMPANY

Above: Quite one of the most dignified and effective of formal bodies is carried by this 1928 Lincoln. The sweep of the front fender makes the sidemount look lower set, and the strength of the waistlining, which carries across the dashboard, is masterful. The photograph was taken in London on October 13, 1928 for agents Wood & Lambert. The name of the coachbuilder is not recorded, but Hooper seems likely.

Above: Lincoln cars were not sold in large numbers in Sweden, so this seven-seater convertible by Alexis Kellner of Berlin was very special. Except in France, wood-spoke wheels with detachable rims scarcely survived the first world war, so this brand new car of 1930 already looks very dated. The body too looks very heavy at the back, though the large rear doors must have facilitated access. The whole car can be compared with the similar body on a 1931 Cadillac on page 40 where the wheels are more appropriate and the overall balance much better than this. *(J. Ströman)*

Opposite: From *Schweizer Touring Club*, 4–13 March 1927, a Swiss advertisement (in French) for Lincoln. (F. Hediger)

Above: Edsel Ford visited the Lincoln factory at Hoboken near Antwerp, Belgium, in 1930 and is photographed here in front of a Lincoln model L seven-passenger sedan with V8 engine. *(Y. and J. Kupélian)*

Above: The Brussels Motor Salon in 1938 where two Lincoln-Zephyrs are displayed. *(Y. and J. Kupélian)*

Above: In the last summer before World War II, guests relax at a hotel at Cliftonville, Kent, having arrived in this Birmingham registered Lincoln-Zephyr convertible sedan.

LOCOMOBILE

Above: At the John O'Groats Hotel at the most northeasterly point of mainland Scotland, Hubert Egerton of Norwich, Norfolk, is setting out on his Locomobile steam car at the beginning of December 1900. He successfully completed the journey to the opposite end of Britain, Land's End in Cornwall, where he arrived on December 22. The Clarkson steam condenser was required for steam cars in Britain to prevent the clouds of steam that might otherwise follow the vehicle's progress. It was not used by Locomobile in the United States. Hubert Egerton's company, Mann Egerton, was formed in 1900 as motor car agents and then coachbuilders. In 1909 the firm became agents for Rolls-Royce and since the second world war has been a major automobile distributor.

The photograph is obviously posed, and it may be noticed that the co-driver of the car is not actually lifting the wheelbarrow; rather the photographer has painted out the ends of its legs in his studio! *(R. Grieves)*

Above: An American car at a military camp of the West Kent Yeomanry, outside the tent of 2nd Lieutenant A. V. Drummond. It is believed that the car is a Locomobile of about 1914, in which case it is the longer wheelbase Model 48 rather than the Model 38. The engine would then have been a six-cylinder of 48.6 h.p. The gas bottle on the running board supplied acetylene for the headlamps, while the sidelights were electric. The car is bodied very much in the English taste for a low and sporty look, but this leaves the driver quite unable to see over the steering wheel, so this imposing and very rare car in England would not have been the most pleasant to drive. Locomobiles had abandoned steam propulsion in 1904.

Opposite, bottom: The first car to arrive in Norway was a Benz in 1895, followed by a few more German cars, another Benz in 1898 and a Daimler in 1899, but by 1902 there were still fewer than ten cars in the country. The firm of F. Hiorth started the first Norwegian dealership in 1902.

Here in Norway are two Locomobiles, which the makers called Locosurreys; probably the third car is a Mobile. The cars were to be sold or hired out for public transportation in Holmenkollen, the famous hill near Oslo (which was then called Christiania). Although seated close above super-heated steam, these pioneer travellers needed to be well wrapped up against the cold and would have been fully aware that within twenty miles they would have to stop to replenish the water tanks at a season when liquid water might not be easy to find. *(T. Krogsæter)*

Above: The Locomobile from Bridgeport, Connecticut, made the Model 48 from 1911 through 1929 when the company finally succumbed after two attempts at resuscitation (Hare's Motors and W. C. Durant). This 1917 model is shown in Norway. Lamps and ornamental work for some Locomobiles at this period were by Tiffany studios, and above the headlights are parking lights. After being private cars for rich owners such cars as this had a long life as public transport over the steep hills of the Norwegian west coast. *(T. Krogsæter)*

Marmon

Above and opposite bottom: This advertisement tells us that these 1921 Marmon 34 limousines were sold to the French High Commission for the use of the general staff. The car shown (opposite) here in Paris must be one of the Marmon 34 limousines used by the French High Commission. The car had the unexpected feature of not only a cast aluminum cylinder block (six cylinders) but also aluminum body, hood and radiator shell. Another peculiarity of the vintage Marmon that it shared with the Lexington, the British Armstrong-Siddeley and the French Mors is the running board curved up the front and rear fenders to the height of the chassis top.

134 *Marmon*

Above: This lady returns to her 1929 Marmon Series 78 eight-cylinder 28 h.p. sedan in Greece, having presumably just visited the Temple of Poseidon, visible in the background.

Opposite: A French advertisement of 1929.

8 cylindres en ligne, en conduite intérieure, pour moins de 60.000 francs présente pour le public un tel attrait qu'il n'est pas étonnant de voir les amateurs de belle mécanique se presser en grand nombre autour de la Roosevelt. Ils peuvent également admirer sur ce stand la **8** cylindres Marmon 68, dernière création des usines d'Indianapolis. XXIII° Salon de l'Automobile, Stand 5

• • •

1 Rue de Presbourg - Téléphone : Elysées 58-45

Nice	12, Avenue de Verdun	Seine, S.-&-O., S.-&-M. :
Cannes	Hôtel Carlton	La Voiture Américaine,
Golfe Juan	Garage St-Cristophe	20, Boulevard de Villiers - Levallois
Marseille	49, rue du Village	Tourcoing - 57, rue du Cœur-Joyeux

Alger : Automobiles Marmon Algérie, 10, rue Michelet - Alger
Maroc : Maroc Auto, 75, rue de l'Horloge - Casablanca

8 en ligne **MARMON** et *Roosevelt*

MARQUETTE

MATFORD

Above: Ford set up shop in Bordeaux in southwest France in 1916, moving to Asnières near Paris in 1927. The V8 was priced out by import duties so a merger was negotiated with Mathis who had been active in Strasbourg since the beginning of the century. The new company, called Matford, was formed in 1934, producing cars at both Strasbourg and Asnières. The 1935 cars were identical to the American V8 but were of French design. The Matford was the only V8 made in the country.

This Matford cabriolet dates from 1938 and is parked outside the church of Saint Louis in Vichy in central France. *(C. Rouxel)*

Opposite: To broaden its market in 1929, Buick introduced the Marquette as its small economy line. By mid–1930, Buick realized it could not compete, and so the make died at the end of the year. Here at the time of the Paris Salon 1929, a Marquette four-door sedan is posed, fitted with the optional disc wheels. Below, on wire wheels and fender-mounted spare, a similar car is seen on the curves of the Col de Braus above Monte Carlo during the January 1930 Monte Carlo Rally. The car was the only Marquette in the rally and started from Jassy in Romania. It was driven by M. Butulesco into thirteenth place (there were 87 finishers) and was winner of the 3,000 cc to 5,000 cc class in the hill climb.

Maxwell

Above: This is a 1906/7 two-cylinder model L runabout seen at Esher in Surrey. The Maxwell-Briscoe Motor Company was established in Tarrytown, New York, in 1904 to build Jonathan Maxwell's design. The engine was a two-cylinder 8 h.p. unit mounted at the front, and it had a two-speed planetary transmission.

Above: Because it was first registered in Cornwall in late 1915, this 1916 model Maxwell has the blacked-out wartime headlamp. The Model 25 was Maxwell's only offering at the time and its electric ignition and starter motor would have been most unusual in England. The owner has fitted oil sidelights and one acetylene headlamp as backup, perhaps not thinking that without a working battery his ignition would not work.

Opposite: Probably made in 1911, this is a Model Q Maxwell touring car with 22 h.p. four-cylinder engine. The photograph is British, and the AA badge (Automobile Association) is of the original style that was replaced in 1911. The square coachlamps were normal Maxwell equipment at the time. By 1911 British cars had adopted front doors, and the author can testify as to the comfort and warmth this gives. This Maxwell did not have front doors as standard, but the model would have in 1912.

Above: Most of the cars in this book would have been on the wrong end of a tow rope at some time; this one is a 1917 Maxwell in Norway. *(T. Krogsæter)*

Above: First registered in London in 1922 is this Maxwell Model 25. The year saw several improvements including drum headlights, a higher hood line and flat body waistline with disc wheels as standard. This car has right-hand drive and the new road tax disc on the windshield frame.

Above: A Maxwell 25 in France. The message on the back tells us the occupants are Monsieur Jonet and Aurore. Disc wheels were standard, but these may be French Michelin ones.

MERCURY

Right: A 1939 Mercury two-door sedan is parked before the Vila Viçosa in the Alentejo region of southern Portugal. Designed to be priced between Ford and Lincoln, it was nearer the Ford than the Lincoln. The photograph was taken in December 1943.

Moon

Above: A very English church lych-gate (this was originally a shelter for coffin bearers) is the backdrop for this 1924 Moon tourer. The Moon radiator had a Rolls-Royce–like form but had a pointed rather than flat section at the top. The Moon was an "assembled" car (built of components from various suppliers as opposed to being all built by the company). The Moon 6-40 had six cylinders.

Opposite: The Moon company was dead in 1930, but here is a Belgian advertisement. Moon had tried to create the Diana in 1925 and the Windsor in 1929. This latter created problems in Britain, where the Windsor light car had been made since 1922, and thus for Europe the old name was used, but large cars were not the answer for anyone in 1930. *(A. Vendiesse)*

La nouvelle 6 cylindres
MOON
est sans concurrence

Une mécanique irréprochable
Des carrosseries d'un goût parfait
Des prix intéressants

MODÈLES 6/60 - 6/72 - 8/80

AGENT GÉNÉRAL BELGIQUE ET GRAND-DUCHÉ DE LUXEMBOURG :
Marcel ROULEAU, 9, boulevard de Waterloo (Porte de Namur), BRUXELLES

AGENT RÉGIONAL :
G. JANNE, boulevard de la Sauvenière, LIÈGE

NASH

Top and above: A happy participant in the Rallye d'Ostende in 1930 in Belgium, proud of the dirt on his car, which must be the Nash Six. In the late twenties, the cheaper models used a side-valve engine and the more expensive models used overhead valves. As with so many American cars in Europe, the headlights have been replaced by much larger European ones. *(Y. and J. Kupélian)*

Below is a similar 1930 Nash but with wooden wheels, owned new by Mr. Alfons Lönell of Skeppsta Manor, Södermanland, Sweden, and registered D-844. *(G. Magnusson, the present owner)*

Above: This Nash appeared on the January 1938 cover of the Swedish magazine *Svensk Motor Tidning. (P-B. Elg)*

Opposite, top: This advertisement is included even though the New Orleans was not made in Louisiana but on Orleans Road, opposite Orleans Park, in Twickenham, Middlesex, England. The firm commenced as licensed builders of the Belgian Vivinus car but in 1905 started to concentrate on much larger cars and changed the name to Orleans so as not to be thought American. The advertisement dates from July 1902.

NATIONAL

Above: The car with the plate reading R-457 is a National Sextet of about 1920. The company had begun with electric vehicles in 1901 and gasoline ones from 1903 (then, and for the next five years with round radiators). In 1922 National merged with Dixie Flyer and Jackson, but two years later it was finished. Wire wheels are unusual for this car.

The car with the plate S-196 is a Hudson of 1926 but still without front wheel brakes. Both cars have space for jump seats or three rows of seats, and contain eight people, as does the V8 Cadillac on the left.

Such public transport as these cars changed life for those on the west coast of Norway. With the country's fjords and mountains, getting from one village to the next had previously involved boat travel out of one fjord and into the next one. Big cars took people and mail over the mountains. *(C. Rogers)*

New Orleans

Oakland

Right: This 1926 six-cylinder Oakland sedan was used as a hire car in the Shetland Islands, which are over 100 miles northeast of John O'Groats in Scotland. The car was operated by Leask & Sons of Lerwick who are still in business today as coach and taxi proprietors. This photograph was taken in 1929 outside the Raewick Hotel in Lerwick. (R. Grieves)

148 *Oakland*

Above: The Oakland All American Six roadster is driven here by Mademoiselle Brémond d'Art, accompanied by her very large dog. The occasion is a Parisian concours d'élégance in 1929. *(H. Roger Viollet)*

Opposite, top: Posed at the time of the Paris Salon of 1926 is this two-door Oakland Sedan with six-cylinder 15 h.p. engine.

Opposite, bottom: An Oakland Six All American four-door sedan. The "W" on the license plate indicates a French trade number, and the car probably dates from 1927.

150   *Oakland*

Above: The next owner of the Oakland All American six pictured on the previous page had lesser ideas of elegance and a lesser dog. The car has been stripped of its fenders, running boards and spare wheels. The date is still only the month of June 1929.

Opposite, bottom: A postcard from Odessa sent to Mr. Tamlin in Twickenham, west of London, in early 1909 depicts an Oldsmobile. One wonders what was advertised in "Poultry Record" that prompted the correspondence.

OLDSMOBILE

Above: An Oldsmobile of 1903/04 in Denmark on a postcard sent to Maria Rasmussen, Prisunds Haspitalet, Copenhagen. Y 87 is its registration number.

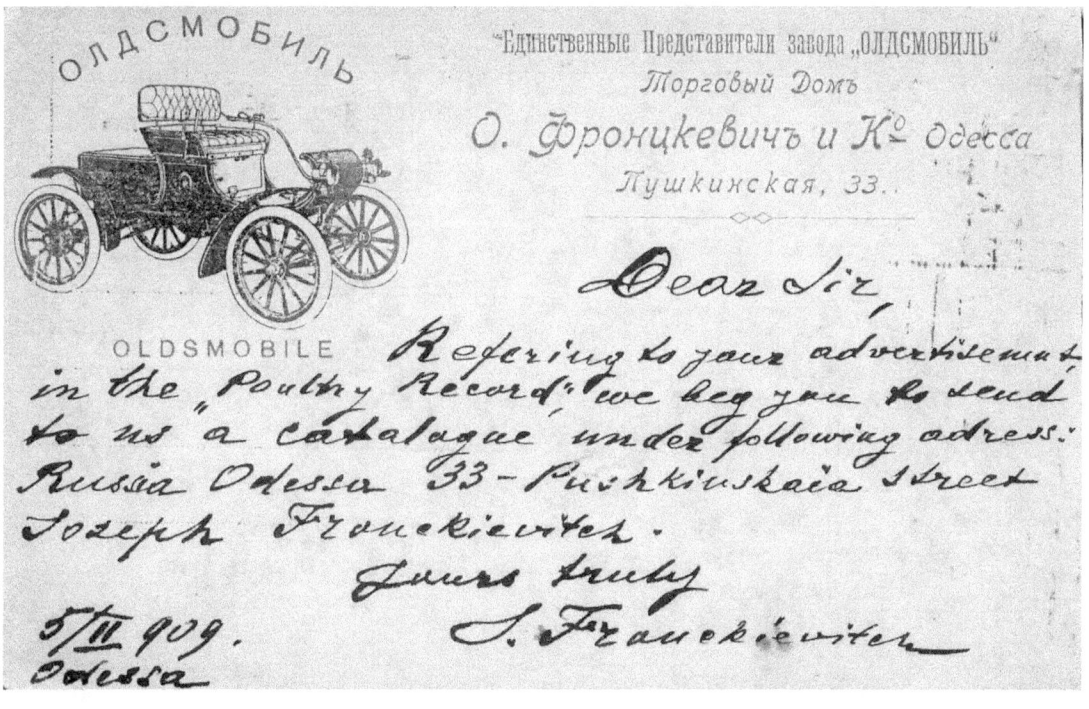

Above: A very happy couple in a 1926 Oldsmobile 30-DT tourer at Ammendorf in Germany. Over two-thirds of this model were exported, this being a first for Oldsmobile. The tourer was the cheapest car in the range at $875 and was sold without bumpers. *(C. Rogers)*

OVERLAND

Above: Overland cars from just before and just after the first world war. *Top, left:* The first is advertised by Pilter-Overland in Paris. *Top, right:* The second is pictured in Sweden *(S. Nyberg)*. *Bottom, left and right:* The third is pictured in Spain and the fourth in Italy.

Right: A Parisian photographer took this picture of what must be an Overland demonstration vehicle, with smart chauffeur in buttoned boots and leather leggings. He appears to be holding a horn bulb with dangling tube. If this had just come adrift from the car he would surely have hidden it. Perhaps it is the remote control for the camera shutter if he took the photograph himself.

Opposite, bottom: Photographed during the Paris Salon of 1928, an F28 model two-door sedan Oldsmobile but with French Michelin wheels.

Above: The Belgian Motor Show at Antwerp in 1921 or 1922 showing the Overland stand. The "Pneu Englebert" sign advertises Belgian-made Englebert tires. *(Y. and J. Kupélian)*

Above: The German-sounding town of Hartmannswillerkopf is in French Alsace near Mulhouse. After nearly 50 years being annexed to Germany, Alsace was returned to France in 1919. Outside the Cantine-Restaurant du Vieil Armand is a 1921 Overland Model 4 Touring showing well its front half-round apron which hides the two transverse quarter elliptic front springs. The registration looks to be British but this seems too unlikely.

Above: A pair of Overlands in Norway with, on the left, a 1922 Model 4 Touring. On the right is an Overland Model 75 Tourer of about 1916. *(T. Krogsæter)*

Above: This example of Overland is from 1924 and in Essex, England. It has the diagonal quarter elliptic front springs of all the 1920s Overlands, and this one is fitted with Dunlop detachable steel artillery wheels and a presumably English tourer body.

156 *Overland*

Above: A change of radiator cannot disguise the front apron of this circa 1924 Overland Tourer seen near Stockholm, Sweden. It is the Model 92 "Redbird." *(S. Nyberg)*

PACKARD

Above: A 1920 Packard with all-weather body by Brussels coachbuilder d'Ieteren delivered on December 20, 1920, to Mr. Englebert of the tire company. *(© d'Ieteren Gallery, Brussels)*

Above: A 1926 Packard Eight that was used by the Directors of the Swedish State Railroads. Originally this Packard was a factory-built seven-seater phaeton. It was rebuilt into this Coupe de Ville by Karosseri AB Norrmalm in Stockholm. *(J. Ströman)*

Opposite, bottom: A four-cylinder model 91 Overland would not be everyone's choice as a racing car, but here is one ready to start on the 24 Hour Race at Francorchamps, south of Brussels in Belgium. *(Y. and J. Kupélian)*

Top and above: A Worcestershire-registered Packard of 1928, photographed on two occasions and with two formalities of pose. The upper photograph is in England while the lower photograph shows an Alpine holiday, probably in Switzerland.

Opposite: An advertisement in the *Revue Touring Club de Suisse* during the Geneva Salon in March 1927. Surprisingly, the statue shown is Nelson's Column in Trafalgar Square, London. *(F. Hediger)*

160 *Packard*

Left: French advertisement for Packard, 1930. "Packard presents a combination of mechanical perfections that cannot be found in any other automobile."

Opposite, top: Although shown here in British Columbia, this is a Packard Super Eight of 1929 bodied as a landaulette by Barker of London. What a very ordinary body from the hands of this coachbuilder "by Appointment to HM the King and HRH the Prince of Wales." Maybe it is the lack of a bottom moulding to the body, and the fact that the top waist moulding is too high set to run forward into any bonnet line, that combine with the sun visor to make it look so prosaic and dull.

Above: In 1930 Mr. Axel Joencke, the Danish consul-general in Stockholm, ordered this cabriolet body on a new Packard 740 chassis. The body was designed by a seventeen-year-old pupil in upper secondary school. The talented young designer later became an architect. He had obviously closely studied German cabriolet bodies of that time. The body was built by Karosseri AB Norrmalm in Stockholm. This huge car attracted much attention during Mr. Joencke's business travels in Europe. In 1936 Mr. Joencke ordered another cabriolet body from Norrmalm for a new Packard V12 chassis, and this latter car is owned today by an American Packard collector.

The size of this drop-head Packard of 1930 is only given away by the four door hinges indicating its considerable weight. The pale molding is on the fat side for European cars, but this car carries it well. One would expect the top of the Swedish bodied Eight Series car to be fully lined against the winter cold. *(J. Ströman)*

Above: A Standard Eight, Ninth Series 1932/33 Packard in the Bois de Boulogne, Paris. The date is September or October 1935, and the personages are actress Lili Palmer, Charles Penrose and the grateful concierge of the restaurant. The background was the making of a Gainsborough picture at Islington Studios in London called *Bad Blood*.

Above: The long hood of this 1933 Packard Eight 5,228 cc convertible by Hermann Graber of Wichtrach, Berne, Switzerland, carries this two-door convertible well, but the low trunk has necessitated the fitting of another and bigger one on the luggage rack. As with other Swiss, German and Czech coachbuilt convertibles, the top would be fully lined and in spite of its low start position would be very bulky when folded. *(F. Hediger)*

Above: Packard built this Twelve in 1934 bodied as a sport phaeton by Rollston Co. of New York. It was built for the king and queen of Yugoslavia.

Above: A 1935 Packard Super Eight with a four-door cabriolet body built by Karosseri AB Norrmalm in Stockholm. Unfortunately Norrmalm's archive was destroyed by fire in 1948, so today nobody can tell who ordered this beautiful car. Norrmalm started in 1919 and made their last non-commercial body in 1938. It was built on a Mercedes-Benz 540 K chassis and still exists in the United States.

This is the third Swedish-bodied Packard in this book and again a very successful design of convertible on a 1935 car. The disappearing waistline complements the beautifully contoured top, which gives an "airline" shape but, as with most convertibles of the period, the top was certainly horsehair lined against the winter cold and would not have folded tidily. *(J. Ströman)*

164 *Packard*

Top and above: These photographs are French, but the car's coachbuilder is not recorded.

Opposite, bottom: This is a 1937 two-door sedan Packard six-cylinder car on a photograph printed in Brussels advertising the Colonial Lottery. *(C. Rogers)*

Above: Here is a 1936 Packard V12. It is a 14th Series, Model 1407, five-passenger coupe. The following year the two doors would become front hinged. The car carries a diplomatic plate. The location is the Place de la Concorde in Paris with the cars in the background entering the Tuileries Gardens towards the Louvre. The 3,200-year-old Luxor obelisk in the center of the square was presented to King Louis-Philippe of France as a gift from the viceroy of Egypt (who also donated Cleopatra's Needle in London). *(H. Roger Viollet)*

PEERLESS

Above: Three American racers were entered for the 1903 Gordon Bennett Race in Ireland; two were Wintons, and this one, a Peerless. They were all from Cleveland, Ohio. This car was driven by L. P. Mooers, but none of the American cars completed the race. *(T. Harding)*

Opposite: A French advertisement for Peerless in 1930.

4 OCTOBRE 1930 — L'ILLUSTRATION — ANNONCES — LXXIX

LA NOUVELLE PEERLESS
S'IMPOSE EN EUROPE

La plus vieille marque américaine de voitures de luxe en progrès ascendant depuis la fin du siècle dernier.

3 MODÈLES 8 CYLINDRES EN LIGNE

Peerless, la seule marque ayant exposé au Salon international d'Amérique pendant 30 années consécutives depuis la vulgarisation de l'automobile, atteint aujourd'hui la perfection grâce aux efforts d'une direction jeune et active et à la classe de ses nouvelles productions qui expriment, plus que jamais, tout ce qu'implique le mot "PEERLESS", synonyme de "sans égal".
La Peerless Motor Car Corporation s'intéresse vivement à la diffusion de ses voitures en Europe, certaine qu'elle est de satisfaire en tout point l'élite des amateurs.
Vous pourrez tout à loisir examiner les trois nouveaux modèles, dont l'éloge n'est plus à faire, en visitant le Stand N° 90 au Salon (Grand Palais) et le Magasin d'Exposition du distributeur pour la France.

AUTOMOBILES PEERLESS (FRANCE)   **63, CHAMPS-ÉLYSÉES, PARIS**

MAGASIN D'EXPOSITION :
12, RUE DE BERRI
Tél. : Élysées 85-30 et 56-45

Directeur Général pour l'Europe : COLDWELL S. JOHNSTON
4, Place de la Concorde, Paris
Télégrammes : Peermotor, Garritus, Paris

PEERLESS MOTOR CAR CORPORATION, CLEVELAND, OHIO. U. S. A.

Pierce-Arrow

Top and above: A model 48 Pierce-Arrow vestibule suburban must have been a rare sight in 1919, so these pictures probably show the same car before and after acquiring a front bumper and losing a big spotlight. The woodland photograph is said to be at Vienna. The second photograph is dated January 22, 1921, and shows the chauffeur Louis Pedeboeuf of the "Commission de Contrôle de Transport Etat Major du deuxième Bureau de la Mayenne, Sector Postale 77." It was taken outside the Reichstag in Berlin.

Above: One of America's finest makes, a Pierce-Arrow in Gothenburg, Sweden. This is a 1925 Model 33 two-seater with rumble seat. Until 1928 only six-cylinder cars were produced. The Dual Valve Six had a T-head engine with four valves per cylinder.

Behind the Pierce-Arrow is a Buick Touring of the same date. It was intended as a seven-passenger model, though it was said that with the jump seats in use, rear seat legroom was inadequate. *(S. Nyberg)*

Above: A French-registered Pierce-Arrow of 1929/30 with the usual New York and European option of separate headlights.

Les nouvelles créations Pierce-Arrow au Salon

Les connaisseurs les plus difficiles et les plus sceptiques ont reconnu, eux-mêmes, la valeur incomparable des splendides nouvelles Pierce-Arrow "Huit". Vous la constaterez à votre tour. Trente ans d'expériences et d'études, soutenues par les principes du traditionnalisme le plus sévère et du modernisme le plus éclairé ont amené les Pierce-Arrow à la perfection. C'est ainsi qu'à été créée la plus belle et la meilleure des voitures américaines. Seule une telle voiture, supérieure en tous points, était à même de gagner la confiance des "leaders" des milieux officiels et mondains, dans tous les pays du monde.

En visitant le Salon, ne manquez pas de vous arrêter au Stand 84. Vous éprouverez un réel plaisir à examiner ces derniers spécimens des créations de Pierce-Arrow qui établissent sa supériorité, soit pour la technique, soit pour la présentation, le confort et le luxe. Faites mieux encore ; confiez à un essai d'une de ces merveilleuses voitures le soin de vous convaincre de leur valeur incomparable.

A.P.A.S. France S/A

au Salon : Stand 84   ou   150, Champs-Elysées

PIERCE-ARROW

Dans la brillante élite des possesseurs de Pierce-Arrow, figurent tous les Présidents des États-Unis depuis 1908.

PLYMOUTH

Above: This is a 1931 Plymouth PA, but what a pity we do not know the story behind the picture. The car is registered in Spain, and four people wait more or less happily behind a chain barrier.

Opposite: Separate headlights are featured on this French advertisement for the 1930 Pierce-Arrow.

172 *Plymouth*

POPE-TOLEDO

Circuit d'Auvergne. Coupe Gordon Bennett 1905
L'Hirondelle, Paris   18. Tracy (Locomobile) Amérique

Above: The 1905 Gordon Bennett Race was the sixth and last in the series created by American James Gordon Bennett, who established in Paris in 1887 a Continental edition of his father's *New York Herald* newspaper. In 1899 he proposed through the Automobile Club de France a series of races with (among other rules) the stipulation that competing cars must be made in their entirety in the entrants' countries.

The 1905 Race was on the Auvergne Circuit west of Clermont-Ferrand in southern France, and the American team comprised a Locomobile and two Pope-Toledos. This photograph is wrongly captioned as Joe Tracy's Locomobile. It is actually Herbert H. Lyttle's Pope-Toledo, which carried No. 6 in the race; the "18" seen on the front of the car is written on the photographer's negative and not on the car. Notice that the front cross-member of the chassis is broken. This car was the last of the twelve finishers and the only American car to finish.

Opposite: At top, Swedish actor Einar Axelsson at the Royal Dramatic Theatre in Stockholm stands beside his new 1934 Plymouth de Luxe Coupe, while below, Rut Holm, popular comedienne of the day, stands beside her 1936 Plymouth de Luxe Cabriolet specially fitted with dual sidemounts. The 1934 car was the first Plymouth to have fully skirted front fenders, which were being widely adopted in 1933/34 and so can be used as a dating feature for cars generally. Both pictures would have been taken for the publicity of Gunnar Philipson, then one of the world's largest private car dealers. In 1934 the Plymouth was third most popular behind Chevrolet and Ford. *(Both J. Ströman)*

RAILTON TERRAPLANE

Above: This is the car tested by *The Autocar* magazine in July 1933 and described as the "most interesting new machine, using as a basis the Straight Eight 4-litre Essex Terraplane engine and gearbox, and resulting in a car of extremely low weight and high power with all that implies in the way of acceleration."

The car was conceived by Noel Macklin, who had previously made Invictas at the same premises at the Fairmile, Cobham, Surrey. Reid Railton, who had designed the Bluebird Land Speed Record car, was a consultant and allowed his name to be used. The chassis were supplied by Hudson Essex Motors. The engines were unaltered, but performance was enhanced by lightened overall weight.

The body was by the short-lived coachbuilder John Charles, which was reborn in 1935 as Ranalah and survived as a coachbuilding company until 1939.

Opposite, top: The 1934 Monte Carlo Rally was won by a Hotchkiss; second place went to a Chenard et Walcker and third to a Triumph. Fourth overall was this 1933 Railton-Terraplane. All the first six cars had started from Athens in Greece.

This is a much modified "Berkeley" saloon. The coachbuilders were Motor Bodies and Engineering Co. of Holloway, London. The car's Portuguese owner, F. de Ribeiro Ferreira, first took it home to Portugal for preparation and modification. One can notice that the work included abbreviation of the fenders, larger tires, two spare wheels on special mounts behind rear trunks that completely obscure rearward vision, and more boxes behind the front fenders. A strap is fitted over the hood and two more straps straddle the roof. Three shovels and a fitted scissor-jack below the rear cross-member can also be seen.

De Ribeiro Ferreira went on to be Portuguese champion driver for the year 1934. *(J. Dyson, Railton Club)*

Above: Based on the new Hudson 74 chassis with Railton's modifications is this Claremont drop-head coupé. Made in Surrey, this one has Surrey registration and is posed on the North Downs hills of that county.

RED BUG

Above: The Auto Red Bug was a simple little buckboard using the flexibility of its slatted wooden floor to obviate the need for any road springs. This is the electric version, powered by a Northeast motor (as then used on Dodge car starters). The power was to the right-hand rear wheel and the brake to the other rear wheel. Perhaps not the most practicable of transport.

This Red Bug has had its pedals extended back so that Master Basil Sanderson, aged 2½, of the Selsdon Park Hotel at Sanderstead in Surrey could drive it. The policeman may not be standing in the safest place unless the photograph was posed for the camera. *(M. Morris)*

Left: A couple in another Auto Red Bug competing in a seaside concours d'élégance in France, though it surely cannot be called elegant. Red Bugs were available for hire on fashionable seaside promenades of the late twenties rather as the miniature electric Bugattis were available for children. *(H. Roger Viollet)*

REGAL

Above: The Regal Motor Car Company of Detroit started business in 1908 and in 1910 introduced this roadster of 18/20 h.p. with a four-cylinder engine. Its surprising feature—well shown here—was its underslung chassis located beneath both axles so the front dumb irons had an inverted appearance. These cars were popular in England where they were imported by Seabrook Brothers of Chelsea, London, and marketed as the RMC or Seabrook-RMC.

Above: A 1916 Regal, still with four-cylinder engine but now a conventional chassis. This one is registered in Kent, England, and we are told that aboard "Grey Lady" are "E.R.J., Georgina Perkins, Emi, Emi's mother (Mrs. Clegg) and Enid Iliffe (now Mrs. Wiltshire)."

Reo

Top and above: Two 30 h.p. Reo torpedo roadsters prepared for participation in the 1911 "Tour de France Automobile." The right-hand car in the lower photograph is driven by Fernand Gabriel, a French race car driver since before 1900.

Above: Between 1906 and 1930 the Swedish Kungliga Automobil Klubben (Royal Automobile Club) arranged long reliability competitions in February, which often were very trying for both cars and drivers due to cold weather and deep snow or thaw and deep mud. This picture was taken during the 1926 event, not far from the finish in Stockholm. At the wheel of this 1925 six-cylinder Reo Model T is Mr. Erik Westerberg, a successful motorcyclist, mainly on the saddle of a Harley-Davidson. He also won many victories as a car driver. *(J. Ströman)*

Above: Registered in Belfast and operated by O'Neil of Bangor, County Down, Northern Ireland, is this 1926 Reo commercial chassis fourteen-seat charabanc about to set out on an excursion. These neat little vehicles, in appearance not unlike a large private car, were popular tour vehicles and were often given names; this one has been christened "The Tonic." *(R. Grieves)*

Above: A group enjoys the seaside in Sweden with a 1928 Reo sedan as their transport. *(C. Rogers)*

SCRIPPS-BOOTH

Opposite, bottom, top and above: In 1912 James Scripps-Booth started making a series of strange cars in his home city, Detroit. In 1915 came the Model C advertised as a "luxurious light car." The floor inside was below the chassis frame. A nickel-silver radiator and Houk wire wheels were good features, but the engine proved to be unreliable. Many were exported, and here are examples in France *(opposite)* and Norway *(top and above)*. *(T. Krogsæter)*

Spacke

Star

Opposite, top: This funny little thing is a Spacke, made in Indianapolis in 1919 and 1920 only. It had a two-cylinder air-cooled engine and two-speed planetary transmission driving the right-hand rear wheel only. It only ever had two bucket seats on the bare chassis, and the later cars, such as this one, were identifiable because the gas tank was moved from the back of the car to a position resembling a "radiator." That such an ephemeral cyclecar should have a sales agent in Belgium, where this one is registered, is astonishing. *(Y. and J. Kupélian)*

STEWART

Above: Stewart Motor Corporation of Buffalo, New York made light- and medium-duty commercial vehicles from 1912 until the beginning of the second war. This is a model 41X ¾ ton of 1933 and working in Norway. *(T. Krogsæter)*

Opposite, bottom: A Star in Norway, 1925. Star was another creation of W. C. Durant when he finally left General Motors in 1920 and was a very successful and low-priced car almost competing with the Model T Ford. For England and the British Empire, the Star was marketed as the Rugby so as not to be confused with the products of British Star Engineering Company of Wolverhampton. In 1928 the Star became the Durant 55 before production ceased. *(T. Krogsæter)*

STUDEBAKER

Above: In 1913 Tyson's Garage at Selby in Yorkshire were agents for Studebaker and for what they called Studebaker Flanders cars. In this photograph, two 1913 Studebaker EC-6 touring cars are parked outside Tyson's. The year 1913 was the last year in which all Studebaker cars were right-hand drive. The message on the back of this postcard reads: "It is quite possible that I shall be out on tour tomorrow, so if I can manage it, I will finish up at York in the evening so will give you a call at the usual time." The garage still stands. *(S. Skilbeck)*

Above: A 1914/15 Studebaker SD-4 Touring with Plymouth, Devon, registration.

Opposite, bottom: A postcard advertising the 1914/15 Studebaker SD-4 Touring. It brings memories of the first world war being addressed to a Henry Coker in the "Kelling Sanatorium" in Norfolk and reads, "We was very pleased to hear from you and also to hear you are getting on so well...."

186 *Studebaker*

Above right: The Studebaker EG Special Six of 1920–1922 seven-passenger sedan was still not big enough for one English customer, who had this extra spacious limousine body made. The principle of seating all occupants within the wheelbase was ignored here. *Above left:* Another Studebaker Special Six is seen in Gothenburg, Sweden. *(S. Nyberg)*

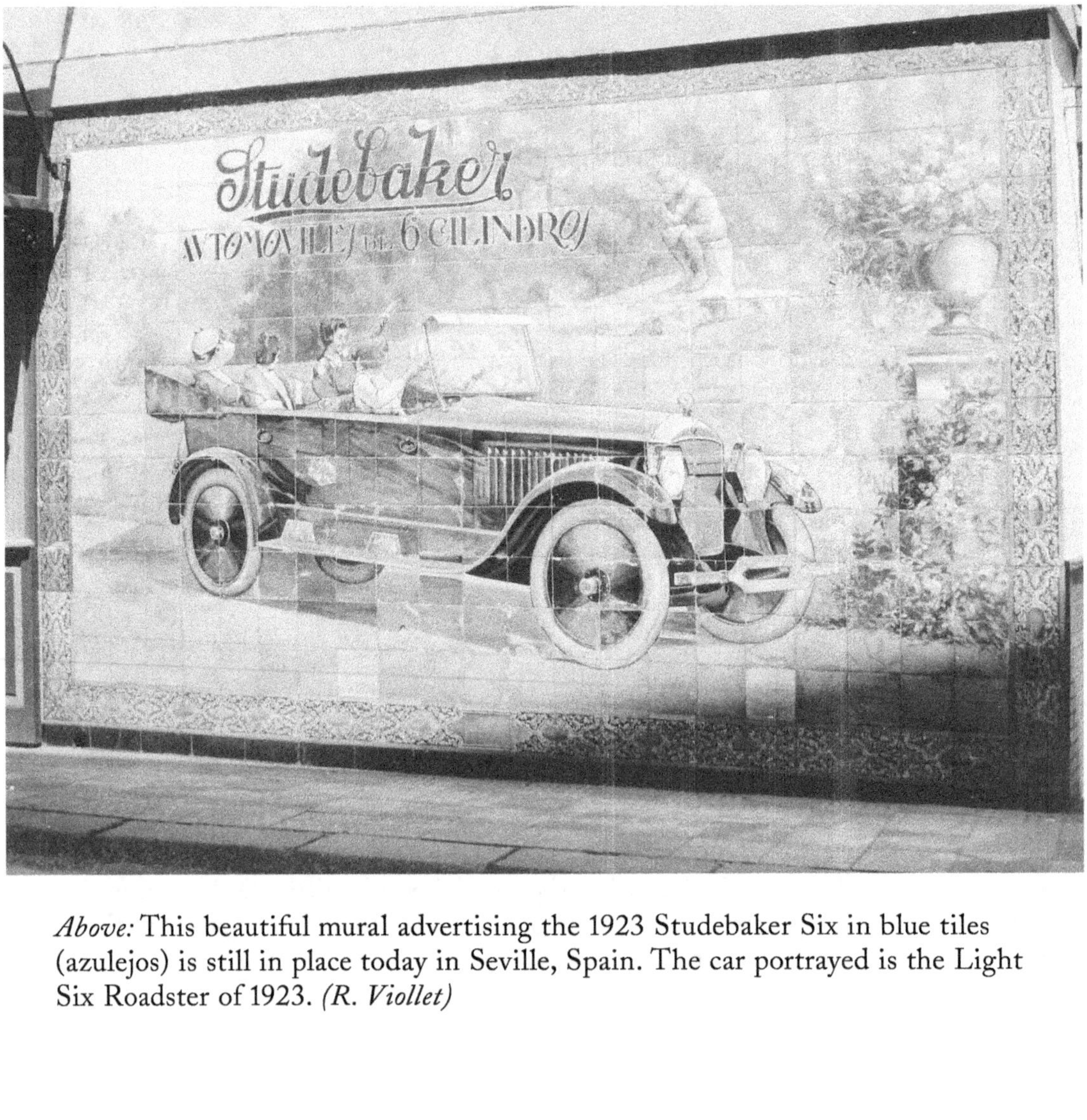

Above: This beautiful mural advertising the 1923 Studebaker Six in blue tiles (azulejos) is still in place today in Seville, Spain. The car portrayed is the Light Six Roadster of 1923. *(R. Viollet)*

Above: Studebaker advertisement for Spain reads, "That's our car!"

ÉLÉGANCES

Le Coupé Pierre-Arrow, écrin de l'élégance, triomphe à la ville comme il règne sur la route.

Vos robes du bon faiseur, vos bijoux précieux, votre personnalité, toutes vos élégances, Madame, demandent l'écrin somptueux qu'est une voiture Pierce-Arrow.

Sa distinction domine sans effort ni extravagance les réunions mondaines les plus choisies.

Limousine somptueuse, gracieux coupé ou alerte torpédo, elle est le fauteuil magique dans lequel vous vous délassez en courant le monde au gré de votre fantaisie.

Des plus coûteuses, elle ne l'est qu'en proportion de ses qualités.

AU SALON STAND N° 88

PIERCE-ARROW

AUTOMOBILES STUDEBAKER
113, Rue Anatole-France, 113
LEVALLOIS (Seine)
Téléphone : Wagram 64-09
SALON D'EXPOSITION : 136, CHAMPS-ÉLYSÉES
Studebaker Pierce-Arrow Export Corporation, South Bend, Indiana (U.S.A.)

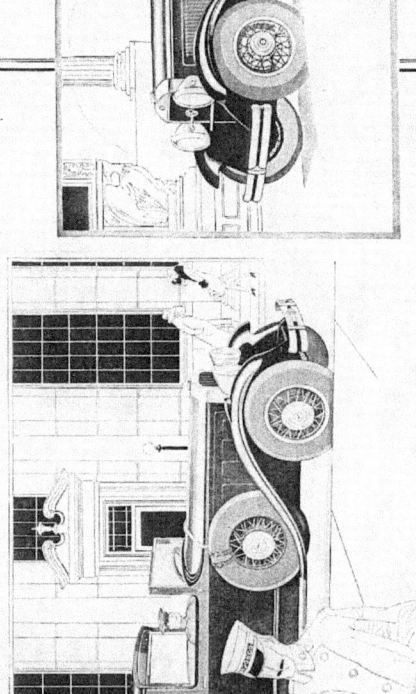

LA PRESIDENT 8 21 177 CV
LA COMMANDER 8 21 117 CV
LA DIRECTOR 8 21 117 CV

Studebaker construit également la "Director". Six pour les automobilistes qui demandent à leur 8me voiture de chasse à un prix moins élevé que celui d'une voiture de luxe.

Venez apprécier la performance
d'une Studebaker "huit-en-ligne"

Studebaker vend plus de voitures huit cylindres qu'aucun autre constructeur. Pourquoi ? Parce que la "President" et la "Commander", dans des performances inégalées, ont conquis à Studebaker plus de records du monde et de records internationaux que n'a détenu aucune autre marque.

Aujourd'hui la nouvelle "Director" huit-en-ligne que présente Studebaker réalise le rêve de l'automobiliste qui ne pourrait posséder jusqu'ici qu'une six cylindres. Vendue à un prix plus bas que celui de la plupart des six cylindres de classe, la nouvelle "Director" toutes les qualités de performance, de confort et de luxe qui ont l'apanage exclusif de la voiture huit cylindres en ligne.

Adressez-vous à l'Agent Studebaker. Prenez le volant d'une Studebaker huit-en-ligne. Ce sera pour vous une véritable révélation.

AU SALON : STAND N° 84

AUTOMOBILES STUDEBAKER
113, Rue Anatole-France, 113
LEVALLOIS (Seine)
Téléphone : Wagram 64-09
SALON D'EXPOSITION : 136, CHAMPS-ÉLYSÉES

STUDEBAKER

Studebaker Pierce-Arrow Export Corporation, South Bend, Indiana (U.S.A.)

Above: G. Gangloff SA of Geneva built this roll-top sedan on a 1929 Studebaker. Studebaker built a plethora of models in 1929 with both six- and eight-cylinder engines. Wire wheels were standard on the Regal but were an option on other models. *(F. Hediger)*

Above: 1934 was another financially bad year, and Studebaker reduced its range from 48 to 8 models, of which this is the three-passenger Commander 8 Coupe with eight cylinders. Here are two of them with French trader's plates at a concours d'élégance. White-wall tires have always been a feature associated by Europeans only with American cars. The side-mounted tire on this car was at extra cost.

Opposite: A 1929 French advertisement. In 1928 the Studebaker Corporation had merged with Pierce-Arrow to give access to the top end of the market. Shared sales premises in Paris was one of the economies, but Studebaker still declared bankruptcy in 1933. The receivers sold Pierce-Arrow and set the company on course for another twenty years.

Above: Sodomka was perhaps the best known of Czechoslovakian coachbuilders specializing in convertible bodies such as this on a Studebaker chassis of 1934. *(National Technical Museum, Prague)*

Above: A stand full of Studebakers at the Brussels Salon in 1938 with a President Convertible Sedan (selling in the United States for $1,385) in the foreground. New for 1938 was Planar independent suspension, referred to as the "Miracle Ride." *(Y. and J. Kupélian)*

STUTZ

Top and above: In Norway, Stutz Tourers from just after the Great War. The top one is followed by a Buick. *(T. Krogsæter)*

192 Stutz

Above: The "Safety Stutz" was introduced in the last days of 1925. It had a straight eight engine with overhead camshaft and double spark plugs per cylinder, hydraulic brakes of new construction, a low center of gravity and was a fast car. In a race in Sweden, a Safety Stutz with a special body beat a 12-cylinder Delage racing car. At the wheel of this open 1927 Stutz is Mr Lamby, in those days a well-known dentist and motorcar enthusiast in Stockholm. His car has Zeiss headlamps, a direction indicator above the number plate and the usual sphinx mascot. *(J. Strömän)*

Opposite, top and bottom: Two anglicized Stutzes. The wire wheels helped their transformation as wooden wheels were not used after 1914/18 on British cars. The saloon even sports a griffon mascot from an early twenties Vauxhall car, though the usual Stutz mascot was a sphinx.

Above: Three Swedish misses in a 1929 Blackhawk, a make created by Stutz of Indianapolis (and lasting until 1929 and 1930) to be a less expensive Stutz. It would be a lovely car to own today, whether with the six-cylinder 85 h.p. engine (3956 cc) or the optional straight eight. This car is still with a Swedish collector and has the eight-cylinder Continental engine. *(J. Strömän)*

THOMAS

Right: Map showing route of the 1908 *Le Matin* race from New York to Paris.

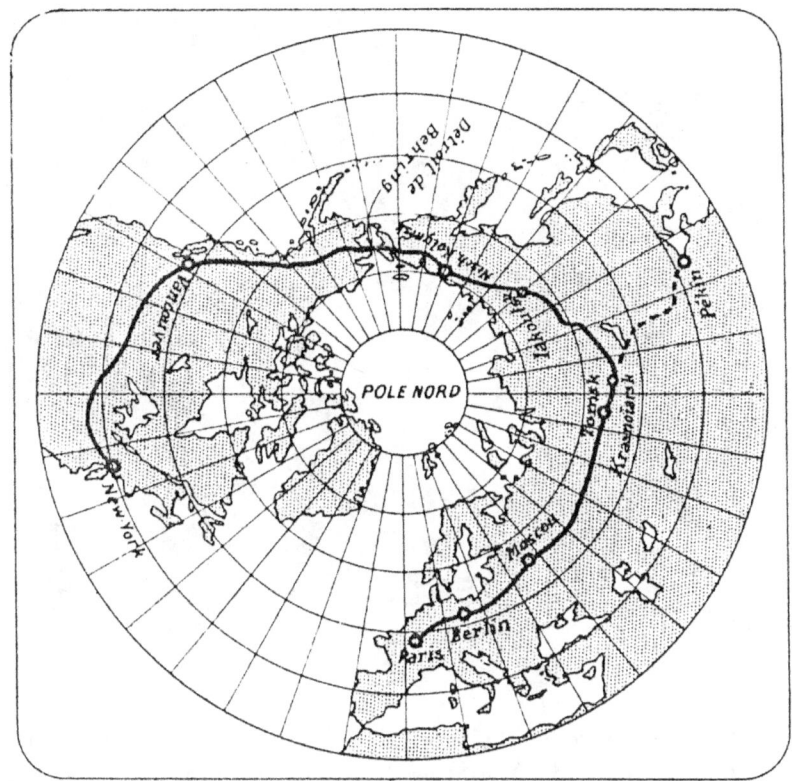

ITINÉRAIRE DE NEW-YORK A PARIS.

Opposite, bottom: In 1907 the Paris newspaper *Le Matin* had promoted a motorcar adventure from Peking to Paris. The only keen participant was an Italian, Prince Borghese, who entered an Itala car. The thought that a foreign team could win a French-sponsored event galvanized the French into participation, but the Italian car still took the honors.

Soon after, *Le Matin* announced the idea for a race (1907 was not supposed to be a race but rather a reliability trial) right around the world from New York to Paris. Regulations were drawn up but altered many times during the event, which was fraught with terrible Arctic weather and a complete absence of roads in most of China and Russia.

This Thomas Flyer of 60 h.p. was entered by its makers. Two wooden planks, the length of the car, doubled as fenders and de-ditching or bridging gear. The journey of some 13,000 miles, most of it where there were no roads, wreaked terrible damage to the cars. Here the car is seen in Paris after the race. The driver is George Schuster, who worked for the Thomas company and was soon promoted from mechanic to driver and captain. On the left is George MacAdam, reporter from *The Times*, and the front passenger is George Miller, a mechanic from the Thomas factory. The other two are not identified. Five days later the car was shipped from Le Havre, northern France, to New York. *(H Roger Viollet)*

WESTCOTT

Above: A short-lived (1916–1925) assembled car from Richmond, Indiana, and then Springfield, Ohio, was the Westcott. This early twenties Model B-44 with six-cylinder Continental engine was photographed in Norway. The luggage guard fitted to the edge of the running board was an accessory more often seen on Model T Fords. *(T. Krogsæter)*

WESTINGHOUSE

Opposite, bottom and above: Carmaking by the Westinghouse Electric and Manufacturing Company took place briefly in 1901 and then for some years from 1905 when a four-cylinder chassis was offered. The car was designed in Pittsburgh but built at Le Havre on the northern coast of France by the Société Anonyme Westinghouse, so was it American or French?

A side view of a 1908 Westinghouse with "tulip double phaeton" body by Th. Botiaux of Levallois-Perret, Paris. This is obviously the coachbuilder's photograph of a new car fitted with canvas seat covers. Behind the chain-driven rear wheels is the luggage rack with coiled leather straps.

Above: This one has Paris registration (I), but there is no information given. The tops on cars of this period did not attach to the tops of the windshield, which is just as well as this car does not have a windshield, but leather straps tensioned the top forward to the tops of the fenders to the hoops shown. *(H. Roger Viollet)*

WHITE

Above: This is a Model B White of 1902 with typically British occupants. One can see how a condenser was incorporated into the production model in the next picture (*below*), which shows a 1903 White.

Above: The year 1905 saw the introduction of the White curved hood line. In this photograph, the considerable depth of the radiator shows that this is in fact a steam condenser. The rear seats of this 1905 White are still accessed from the center of the back of the car, not ideal when the top is furled, but this would be the last year before side doors on the White as on almost all other makes. The registration is from Northamptonshire in England.

Opposite, bottom: It must be coincidence, but this White steam car of 1903 is being offered for sale by Mr. I. P. White, automobile engineer, of 57 King Street, Manchester, England, at a price of £250 in the year prior to the introduction of registration numbers. It was in 1903 that Whites introduced a front-mounted compound engine and the steam condenser placed in the frontal "radiator" position. White made steam cars from 1901 to 1910, when petrol cars were introduced. After 1918, White made only commercial vehicles.

WILLS SAINTE CLAIRE

Above: A very European style D-back limousine on a 1922 Wills Sainte Claire chassis. In this case the coachbuilder, D'Ieteren of Brussels, has also built the fenders, so it is only the wheels that immediately give away the chassis' nationality. The doors are front hung, and the fenders have flowing European lines and "presence." The radiator mascot and radiator logo were patterned on the grey geese that migrated over Harold Wills's home on the banks of the River St. Clair (to which he added an "e" for a bit of class) every spring and autumn.
(© D'Ieteren Gallery, Brussels)

Opposite: The body of the Wills Sainte Claire shown in the previous photograph was built by D'Ieteren Frères of Brussels, to the patents of Charles Weymann. This advertisement explains the "Weymann Principle."

WEYMANN

THE BODY OF TO-DAY AND OF THE FUTURE

The Secret is in the Structure and Air-Space Joints.

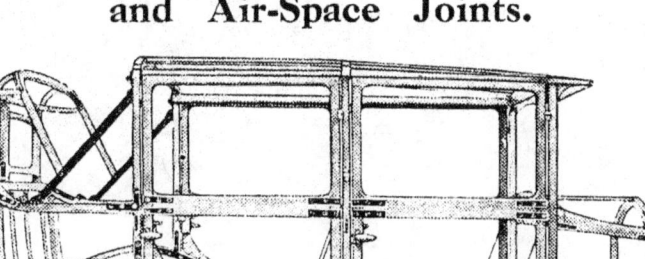

This sign is on the true Weymann Body. Look for it.

A Fabric-covered Body is not a Weymann Body unless it has a Licence Plate.

Seven Advantages of the Weymann Principle.

1. The silence and luxurious comfort.
2. Withstands the worst of road shocks.
3. Cleaning much easier. Car can be put away wet and muddy without risk of damage.
4. Easily and quickly repaired.
5. Paintwork troubles eliminated.
6. Can be obtained on any chassis.
7. Extreme lightness.

Joint Advertisement by the following Makers of Genuine Weymann Bodies

Motor Body Builders:

HORACE ADAMS, Ltd.,
St. Thomas St., Newcastle-on-Tyne

WILLIAM ARNOLD,
105, Upper Brook St., Manchester

J. BLAKE & CO., Ltd.,
35, Hardman Street, Liverpool

CADOGAN MOTORS (1928) Ltd.,
Bishops Road, Fulham, S.W.6

CARLTON CARRIAGE CO., Ltd.,
Waldo Road, Willesden, N.W.10

CAVERSHAM MOTORS Ltd.,
Reading

JOHN CHALMERS & SONS, Ltd.,
50, High Street, Redhill

CHARLESWORTH BODIES, Ltd.,
Coventry

CONNAUGHT MOTOR &
34, Davies St., W.1 [Carriage Co.,Ltd.

FLEWITT, Ltd.,
120, Alma Street, Birmingham

JOHN FOWLER & SONS, Ltd.,
19, York Place, Harrogate

FREESTONE & WEBB, Ltd.,
101-103, Brentfield Rd., Willesden, N.W.10

T. H. GILL & SON, Ltd.,
23, Chilworth Street, W.2

H. A. HAMSHAW, Ltd.,
37, Humberstone Gate, Leicester

HANCOCK & WARMAN, Ltd.,
Brays Lane, Coventry

THOMAS HARRINGTON, Ltd.,
89, Church Street, Brighton

KELLY DAVIES CO., Ltd.,
75, North St., Cheetham, Manchester

W. H. KNIBBS & SONS, Ltd.,
Tipping St., Ardwick, Manchester

LANCEFIELD COACHWORKS,
Wrenfield Place, W.10

MANN, EGERTON & CO., Ltd.,
156 New Bond St., W., & Norwich, Ipswich, &c.

MARSHALSEA BROS., Ltd.,
East Street, Taunton, Somerset

F. MAULE & SON,
Skinner Street, Stockton-on-Tees

MORGAN & CO., Ltd.,
Bridge Street, Leighton Buzzard

MOTOR BODIES & ENGINEERING
39, Hartham Road, N.7 [Co. Ltd.,

MULLINERS, Ltd.,
Bordesley Green Road, Birmingham

ARTHUR MULLINER, Ltd.,
73-83, Bridge Street, Northampton

E. J. NEWNS,
Portsmouth Road, Thames Ditton

J. GURNEY NUTTING & CO., Ltd.,
10a, Elystan Street, Chelsea, S.W.3

PARK, WARD, Ltd.,
473, High Road, Willesden, N.W.

F. W. PLAXTON,
SMITH & BIANCHI, Ltd.,
Castle Works, Scarborough

RIPPON BROS., Ltd.,
Viaduct Street, Huddersfield

UNION MOTOR CAR CO., Ltd.,
19, Denbigh St., Belgrave Rd., S.W.1

MARTIN WALTER Ltd.,
62-64, Sandgate Road, Folkestone

F. J. WILLIAMS,
Berkeley Avenue, Cheltenham

G. WYLDER & CO.,
Station Avenue, Kew Gardens

JAMES YOUNG CO., Ltd.,
Bromley, Kent

Chassis Manufacturers:
HILLMAN MOTOR CAR CO., LTD., Coventry.
LAGONDA LTD., Staines, Middlesex.

Issued by Weymann Motor Bodies (1925) Limited, 47, Pall Mall, London, S.W.1

WILLYS-KNIGHT

Above: Registered in Belgium is this Willys-Knight touring with detachable disc wheels and bumpers as extras. The engine had double sleeve valves from the start in 1914 using the patent of Charles Y. Knight of Wisconsin as also used by Daimler in England, Minerva in Belgium and others.

Above: A Norwegian lady shows off her 1931 Willys-Knight 98-D sedan. The car was one of the last to use the Knight sleeve-valve engine of six cylinders, and it was made while John Willys was absent from his Toledo factory as America's first ambassador to Poland (1930–1932). *(T. Krogsæter)*

Opposite, bottom: A potato wholesaler's 1929 Willys Knight parked outside a cigar importer's in Gothenburg, Sweden. *(S. Nyberg)*

Winton

Above: Two Winton racing cars were brought from Cleveland, Ohio, to Ireland for the Gordon Bennett Race of 1903. One was an eight cylinder, comprising two four-cylinder horizontal engines claiming a modest 80 b.h.p. from 17 liters to be driven by Alexander Winton; the other was a four for Percy Owen. Here is the latter queuing for the weighbridge in the market place at Naas. Note the big box camera resting on the hood. At the start of the race Winton drove the four-cylinder car, but carburetor trouble prevented him getting away and several competitors had completed their first lap of fifty-eight miles before he started. Neither of the Wintons finished. *(T. Harding)*

Percy Owen's car had four horizontal cylinders and 8,513 cc, while Alexander Winton drove a car with eight horizontal cylinders and 17,016 cc. Neither of the Wintons finished. *(T. Harding)*

INDEX

Ades, Mr. 74
Ajax 8
Alberts (garage) 74
Alfonso XIII (King of Spain) 36
Alsace 154
Ammendorf, Germany 152
Amsterdam, Holland 47
Antwerp, Belgium 47, 154
Armstrong-Siddeley 132
Arras, France 88
Asnières, France 137
Atcherley, W.C. 13
Athens, Greece 174
Auburn 55, 110
Audi 92
Augustendal, Sweden 69
Auto Union 92
Auvergne, France 173
Axelsson, Axel 173

Bad Blood (film) 162
Barker & Co. 161
Batignolles, Paris, France 87
Bedford/Buick 7, 14, 48
Bedfordshire 112
Belfast, Northern Ireland 179
Belgium 35, 37, 47, 55, 66, 74, 80, 95, 108, 125, 128, 144, 154, 157, 183, 202
Benz 3, 131
Bergstrom, Clemens 55
Berlin, Germany 25, 40, 70, 72, 127, 168
Berne, Switzerland 19, 25, 56, 162
Berns, Paul 62
Birmingham, England 13, 129
Bluebird 174
Bonnie and Clyde 99
Bordeaux, France 137
Botiaux, Th. 196
Bournemouth, England 108
Brémond d'Art, Mlle. 149
Bridgeport CT 132
Bridgewater, England 80
Briscoe, Benjamin 8
British Columbia 161
Brussels, Belgium 35, 37, 67, 73, 74, 128, 157, 190, 200
Buda 29
Budapest, Hungary 97

Buffalo NY 183
Bugatti 73, 175
Buick 26, 41, 73, 101, 110, 125, 169, 191
Butulesco, M. 137

Cadillac 19, 26, 125, 127, 146
Cannes, France 12, 58, 72, 101
Cardiff, Wales 81
Castagna 60
Champs Elysées, Paris, France 23
Charles, John 174
Chenard et Walcker 95, 174
China 195
Chrysler 65, 110
Citroen 99
Clemenceau, G. 33
Clermont Ferrand, Frnce 173
Cleveland OH 106, 204
Cliftonville, England 129
Closser, Louise 7
Coder 96
Columbia axle 121
Columbus OH 120
Continental 8, 67, 77, 194, 196
Copenhagen, Denmark 151
Cord 69
Cornwall, England 115, 130, 139
Coventry, England 76
Czechoslovakia 53, 190

D.K.W. 69, 92
D.S. 67
Daimler 3, 85, 131, 202
Davies, Dolly 116
Delage 58, 73, 95, 192
Delahaye 73, 95
Delaunay-Belleville 95
Denmark 8, 106, 157, 161
Detroit 67, 106, 181
Dewaet 67
D'Ieteren Frères 35, 74, 157, 200
Dijon, France 86
Dixie Flyer 146
Dodge 65, 69
Douglas, Captain 32
Dover, England 57
Dresden, Germany 97
Drummond A J 131
Dunlop 155
Durant 70, 183

Dusseldorf, Germany 94

Earl, Harley 123
Edward VIII (King) 27, 28
Egerton, Hubert 130
Ekman, Gösta 79
Elton, Lord 85
Elyria OH 83
England 33, 36, 53, 64, 69, 74, 76, 81, 84, 85, 109, 112, 120, 139, 142, 159, 186, 192
Englebert Tires 47, 80, 83, 97, 154, 157
Esher, England 138
Essex 110, 155, 174
Ettler 22
Eugen (Prince of Sweden) 99

"Fägel Blä" 60
Ferreira, Ribeiro 174
Fiat 91
Finland, Miss 99
Fisher, Lawrence 123
Flint MI 70
Ford 50, 55, 121, 128, 183, 196
Fordson 94
Fort Augustus Abbey, Scotland 15
Franay 42
France 8, 9, 10, 12, 14, 19, 20, 27, 33, 34, 49, 53, 58, 62, 72, 86, 88, 112, 113, 116, 133, 137, 141, 164, 169, 175, 178, 181, 189
Francorchamps, France 157
Fremont-Mais 29

Gabriel, Fernand 178
Gangloff, G., SA 38, 189
Gebrüder Tüscher & Co. 41
General Motors 26, 48, 51, 76, 123, 125, 183
Geneva, Switzerland 38, 44, 51, 159, 189
Germany 33, 34, 67, 70, 79, 92, 94, 97
Glaser 97
Gordon Bennett Race 166, 173, 204
Gothenburg, Sweden 91, 106, 169, 186
Graber 56
Graber, Hermann 162

205

Index

Graham 55, 69
Graham-Paige 110
Grand Palais, France 23
Grande Cascade Restaurant 18
Grands Garages de Bretagne 95
Grebel 72
Greece 134, 174
Grünewald, Isaac 60
Guildford, England 31
Gustav V (King of Sweden) 99
Gustav Nordbergs 125
Guttman & Gacon (garage) 38

Haga Park, Stockholm, Sweden 30
Hans Osterman AB 39
Hansom Cab 91
Harley-Davidson 179
Harlow, Jean 62
Hartmannswillerkopf, France 154
Heffermehl, Carl 13
Hertfordshire 27
Hewitt, E. R. 7
Hilversum, Holland 74
Hiorth, F. 120, 131
Hispano-Suiza 62, 123
Hoboken, Antwerp, Belgium 128
Holland 98
Holm, Rut 173
Hooper 127
Horch 92
Hotchkiss 174
Houk wheels 181
Hudson 13, 146
Hungary 97
Hupmobile 25, 41

Indianapolis IN 183
Inverness, Scotland 15, 32
Invicta 174
Ireland 166, 179, 204
Itala 195
Italy 153

Jackson 146
Jackson MI 8
Jassy, Romania 137
Joencke, Axel 161
John O'Groats, Scotland 130, 147
Jönköping 70

Kellner, Alexis 25, 40, 119, 127
Kellner Frères, Paris 40
King Haakon VII, Norway 22
Knight, Charles Y. 202, 203

La Chaux de Fonds, Switzerland 38
Lamby, Mr 192
Lancefield Coachwork 41
Land's End, England 130
Langenthal AG, Carrosserie 25, 119
LaSalle 26, 37
Leask & Sons, Lerwick, Scotland 147
Le Baron 72
Le Havre, France 195, 196
Le Mans, France 53

Letourneur et Marchand 72, 73
Lexington 132
Lillehammer, Norway 13
Lincolnshire, England 14
Lion de Belfort, France 89
Lloyd George, D. 33
Locomobile 173
London, England 7, 9, 16, 35, 36, 41, 58, 62, 70, 81, 85, 88, 91, 127, 140, 177
London-to-Brighton 3, 76
Lönell, Alfons 142
Louisville KY 69
Lycoming 58
Lyddiatt 85
Lyons, France 89

Machade, José 77
Macklin, Noel 174
Manchester, England 85, 89, 199
Mann Egerton 130
Mannheim, Germany 3
Marchal 28, 98
Marseille, France 96
Martin, Bournemouth, England 108
Mathis 137
Matile, H. 95
McAdam, George 195
Mercedes-Benz 69, 163
Michelin 141, 153
Michigan 30
Milan, Italy 60
Miller, George 195
Milnes-Daimler 29
Minerva 68, 202
Mobile 131
Mobiloil 55
Monte Carlo Rally 137, 174
Mooers, L. P. 166
Moon 68
Morris 27
Mors 132
Moskvitch 22
Motor Bodies 174
Murray 16

Naas, Ireland 204
Nash 121
Nelson's Column, London, England 159
Netherlands 74, 77
Neuchatel, Switzerland 38
New Orleans, Twickenham, England 146
New York 62
New York to Paris 195
Nicholas of Romania (Prince) 72, 73
Nilson, Axel 30
Nordberg 26
Nordbergs Vagufabriks AB, Gustaf 39
Norrmalm, Karasseri AB 157, 161, 163
Northamptonshire 199
Northeast 175
Northup, Amos 116
Norway 8, 13, 17, 22, 33, 34, 43, 64, 76, 78, 83, 101,115, 119 125, 131, 132, 140,146, 155, 181, 183, 191, 196, 203
Norwich, England 130
Nottingham, England 13

Oakland 64
Oatlands Park Motor Co 16
Odessa, Russia 150
Oldsmobile 99, 125
O'Neil of Bangor, Northern Ireland 179
Oporto, Portugal 65
Oslo, Norway 120, 131
Osterman, AB Hans 26, 125
Ousby-Trew, Miss W.F.M. 31
Owen, Percy 204
Oxford, England 15

Packard 41
Paige-Detroit 120
Palm Beach Casino, Cannes, France 101
Palmer, Lili 162
Paris, France 18, 23, 33, 37, 42, 58, 60, 72, 87, 89, 91, 95, 118, 123, 149, 153, 162, 165, 196
Peking to Paris 195
Penrose, Charles 162
Philipsons 60, 69, 173
Pierce-Arrow 33, 189
Pilter-Overland 153
Pittsburgh PA 196
Plymouth 65
Plymouth, Devon 185
Poland 203
Portago, Alfonso 73
Portago, Marquis de 73
Portugal 28, 65, 77, 174
Poseidon Temple, Greece 134
Prague, Czechoslovakia 53, 56, 100
Presland's Ltd. 48
Prince Charles 57
Privat 86

Quensel, Isa 69

Railton 13
Ranalah 174
Reading PA 64
Red Flag Act 3
Renault 73, 110
Richmond IN 196
Rochet-Schneider 95
Rock Hill SC 8
Roe, Fred 70
Rolls-Royce 130
Rollston & Co NY 163
Romania, Sucreries and Raffineriès 35
Rosengart 95
Rousset, A. 89
Rugby 183
Russia 195
Rylstone 19

Sanderson, Basil 175
Santander, Spain 110

Index

Saoutchik 37, 60
Saxony, Germany 79
Schuster, George 195
Scotland 15, 32, 78, 130
Seabrook 177
Selby, Yorkshire, England 184
Seville, Spain 186
Shell 74
Shetland Islands, Scotland 147
Sigvard Bernadotte of Sweden 93
Simpson, Mrs Wallis 27
Skoda 22
Smith-King 29
Södermanland, Sweden 142
Sodomka 190
Somerset, England 109
Spain 36, 57, 153, 171, 186
Springfield OH 196
Star (Wolverhampton) 183
Stavanger, Norway 22
Stettin 67
Stockholm, Sweden 26, 30, 39, 69, 79, 93, 100, 125, 155, 157, 161, 163, 173, 179, 192
Stoewer 67
Strasbourg, France 137
Stuttgart, Germany 3
Surrey 16, 175

Svensk Filmindustri 69
Sweden 26, 30, 39, 40, 48, 49, 51, 52, 55, 60, 62, 69, 70, 79, 84, 91, 93, 99, 100, 106, 122, 127, 144, 153, 156, 157, 163, 169, 173, 179, 180, 186, 192, 194, 203
Swedish State Railroads 157
Switzerland 21, 25, 38, 41, 44, 51, 56, 68, 69, 119, 159, 162, 189

Tamlin, Mr, Twickenham 151
Tärnsjö, Sweden 52
Tarrytown NY 138
Tiffany 132
Toledo 203
Triumph 174
Twickenham, England 146
Tyson's Garage 184

Uhlik 53, 56, 100

Van den Plas 73
Västmansland Iän 52
Vauxhall 48, 192
Vernon, Winifred 62
Versailles, Treaty of 33
Vichy, France 137
Victor Emmanuel II (King) 33

Vienna, Austria 168
Vigo Motors 46
Vila Viçosa, Portugal 141
Vivinus 146
Voisin 72
Vörmland, Sweden 48

Wanderer 92
Wartburg 22
Watford 27
Wedel Jarlsberg (Count) 120
West Kent Yeomanry 131
West Lothian, Scotland 78
Westerberg, Erik 179
Weybridge, England 16
Weymann, Charles 89, 200
Whippet 83
Willys, J.N. 83
Wilson, T.W. 33
Wilson, Woodrow 33
Windsor 142
Winton 166, 204
Wisconsin 202
Wolseley 27
Wood & Lambert 127

Zeiss 192
Zurich, Switzerland 41

www.ingramcontent.com/pod-product-compliance
Lightning Source LLC
Chambersburg PA
CBHW081556300426
44116CB00015B/2906